SOMETHING ELSE

by Lukas Simko

*This book was written in silence, when the world couldn't see me.
Not all truths need noise. Some are whispered... when only the stars are awake.*

SOMETHING ELSE

By Lukas Simko.

☉

This book is based on real events and true experiences from the author's life. Some names and identifying details have been changed out of respect for the privacy of those involved.
The feelings, lessons, and moments shared within these pages remain exactly as they were lived.

☉

Cover design by Lukas Simko
Interior design by Natalia Junqueira

☉

Copyright © 2025 Lukas Simko

All rights reserved.

ISBN: 978-1-9191698-0-4

☉

For information, visit: www.somethingelsebook.com

*To my grandparents, Pavlína and Jozef
who taught me that love doesn't end when life does.*

Contents

Prologue - The Happy Soul - 4 1

The Flame That Survived 5

The Spark in the Music 8

The Bridge, Not the Destination 11

The Little Things Along the Way 16

At the Doorstep of Something 20

When the Universe Opens the Door 23

The Promise and the Shadow 32

From Warmth to Winter 37

A New Language, A New Part of Me 43

The Middle of Nowhere, and Everything 47

The Right Time - : 50

The Call That Set Me Free 53

The Girl in the Red Dress 58

When Silence Spoke Back 64

The Day the Universe Brought Us Back 68

Where Something Else Began 72

The One Who Said Yes 75

The Altar I Never Knew I Built 78

A Place of Truth 84

Destiny in Motion 97

Stars in the Sea 99

The Quiet Shine 102

The Invitation 106

When Magic invites you in 110

The Night I Belonged 116

The Last Day in Sicily 120

Epilogue 125

Thank You 128

About the Author 129

Prologue
The Happy Soul
4

I never had a perfect life, but I had a happy one. I grew up surrounded by love from my mama and my nanny. That love shaped me, even when I didn't realise it at the time. It was the kind of love that gave me freedom to laugh, to make mistakes, to dream, to love.

I remember one night, when I was about six or seven, I woke up. It was late. I heard crying. I looked to the other side of the room at my sister, she was sleeping. I got up and followed the sound. It was dark everywhere. I was scared, couldn't see anything, but I walked with my little feet towards her. I knew it was my mama; I knew her voice. The love I carried in my heart, the one she gave me, was stronger than anything in this world. Nothing could stop me from wanting to protect her. When I opened the door, my mama was lying on the edge of the bed. The lamp beside her softly lit the corner where she was, her face turned away, trying not to show her tears.

I didn't know then why she was crying. Only later I learned that while she was carrying us, giving my father all her care and love, everything she had, she had somehow discovered his lies. He wasn't really working late nights… he was spending them holding another woman in his arms. That night, all I wanted was to help her, to stop whatever made her cry, whatever had broken her.

It was the purest love, I wanted to protect my mama with it, the kind of love that never lies or leaves, the kind that still makes you smile when the world hurts. I didn't understand the world yet. I wasn't touched by its bad side, because my mama's love was the only truth I knew.

I asked softly, "Why are you crying, mami?"

She wiped her eyes and said, "I just had a bad day, Luki."

I still remember those eyes, full of tears still trying to smile, trying to protect me even when it hurt her so much.

I climbed beside her, wrapped my arms around her, and said, "I'll stay with you, so you won't feel sad." I remember that warm hug, the strong one she gave me. For a moment it felt like maybe my small promise could hold the world together.

My father's leaving came quietly. I don't remember him leaving, only the silence that followed, nights that grew heavier, quieter. He still taught me something, not through love, but through absence. He gave me the clearest example of who I never wanted to be.

Maybe that's why I've always tried to stay, to listen, to love even when it hurt. Because that night, without knowing it, I made a promise I've kept my whole life, to never make someone feel like they weren't worth staying for.

I think that moment shaped more of me than I ever realised. I grew up trying to be the kind of presence I once needed, gentle, steady, honest. Maybe that's why I never learned how to love halfway. When I care, I care completely. When I stay, I stay with everything.

Sometimes people say I feel too much, but they never saw that moment, the little boy holding his mother, promising her she wouldn't be alone. That promise never left me. It became the way I move through life, the way I hold others, the way I write. Every story I've lived carries a piece of that night, the need to stay, to understand, to heal what leaving once broke.

Even now, after all the people who came and went, after all the love that burned and faded, a part of me still believes in staying, not because it's easy, but because that night taught me how much it matters.

I was never the best at everything, but I had something people seemed to notice. I could make people laugh. I could make them feel, even believe, not in me, but in themselves. Friends gathered around me not because I tried, but because something about me made them stay.

I travelled when I could. I learned from the world, even when schoolbooks never seemed to fit me. I was curious, open, alive. I have always been a happy soul, even when the world hurt, even when some people didn't stay. I laughed with stars and smiled at strangers because joy was mine, not given, but chosen. There was always a spark inside, a little light that kept me going.

Looking back now, I see that those were the roots of who I am, a soul that could be hurt, tested, broken down, but somehow always finds its way back to laughter, to love, to light.

That is who I was.

That is who I still am, beneath everything that happened later.

This isn't a polished life story. It's a lived one.

The Flame ThAt Survived

Life has a way of testing how strong we are.

My life wasn't easy. The older I got, the more I was afraid that I would never find what I had always been looking for. Someone to build a life with, a family, kids. A home filled with love, where we solve problems together and grow side by side. I had a few relationships, and when I didn't, I enjoyed my life. Yet with every year that passed, the thought crept in, *I'm getting older. Maybe I don't have much time left.*

I graduated college at the age of 32 and found it extremely difficult to find work. During my studies I had an accident. I lost my job and couldn't walk. Recovery took two long years, and it affected my grades. My grades certainly weren't perfect, and I just about passed. Most companies weren't interested in someone like me, especially in IT.

In my final year, during the last semester I met someone. I met a girl I thought would love me the way I loved. I won't mention her name, I'm not hiding it, but she doesn't matter anymore. She was only a lesson, nothing more.

She came from a wealthy family and never had to worry about the future. While I was applying for jobs, sending over three hundred applications and receiving rejection after rejection, she said to me, "Maybe you should stop looking in IT. Maybe work in retail instead. Or for my dad. A few days a week, nothing hard. At least then you'd bring some money in, instead of just welfare."

Sometimes love is blind. You don't see what's happening behind the corners. I didn't notice how I was slowly losing myself.

I worked for her family six days a week for over a year, lifting heavy furniture, doing whatever was asked of me and at the same time, she started controlling everything, telling me what to say in front of her parents and her friends. Deciding who could I see and what I should hide. She kept telling me I was wrong, again and again, until I started to believe it.

After working for her dad for a while, I got a job offer in IT. It was far away, but I was happy to finally have a chance to move forward. I was so excited that I told her and her family right away. They congratulated me, and she smiled in front of them however later, when everyone had gone, she looked at me and said, *"If you take this job, we are over and it will be your fault. Because you never think about us, only about yourself."*

From happiness, I fell straight into darkness, overthinking everything. Maybe she was right, maybe it really was my fault. The fear grew from the words she said, so I called the company and rejected the offer. This went on for nearly four years. Four years of slowly losing myself, until I almost believed I was nothing.

That was one of the darkest moments of my life. Pretending everything was okay when inside there was almost nothing left only worry and emptiness. I began to believe I wasn't the good person I always thought I was, yet still, somewhere deeply inside me, I had a little flame left.

One day, on a call with my mama, I reacted in a way I never had before. She said something small, and I jumped straight into defending myself, raising my voice, throwing words back at her like weapons. She stopped me.

"Lukas, what is happening to you? This isn't you. Why are you talking to me like this?"

In that moment, I realised she was right. I wasn't really fighting her. I was fighting everything inside me. I was only defending myself because that was all I had left.

Later, I applied for another job. It wasn't IT, just customer support, far away. I called my friend, desperate, *"Please, tell me what to do, because I don't know anymore."* He told me exactly what I needed to hear.

I took the job. The universe played in my favour. It was during the pandemic, and travel wasn't allowed. She couldn't follow me and this was the beginning of the end. Of course, she sent bad messages, angry calls, screaming who I was and how no one would ever want to be with me.

This time, I didn't break. Darkness ended and the light found me again. I met new people, made new friends, and one of them, Nick, became someone who helped me step back onto the right path. Even when our lives took us in different directions, we stayed in touch.

A year later in 2021, I returned to the town I had once left behind. Maybe the universe wanted to prove a point to show me that because I didn't give up on searching for an IT job, I was finally offered one. Not just anywhere, but right there, in the same place where I'd once been told to give up and work for her family business instead.

When she saw me again, she screamed at me in a car park, throwing her poison but it no longer touched me by then, I knew I was the one in control of my life.

Still, something inside me had changed. I wasn't the same. A part of her stayed in me, and I didn't know how to heal it.

The Spark iN the Music

*E*verything began after a festival in August 2022. A friend of mine, Nick, who is Dutch, was very close to me at the time. We had only known each other for about a year, working together in Dundalk and we become very good friends. He had won a ticket to one of the most sought-after festivals in Europe, *Tomorrowland – The Reflection of Love*. The prize allowed him to invite two friends, and out of everyone he knew, he chose me.

I asked him, "Why did you invite me, out of all your friends?"

He smiled kindly.

"Lukas, I could've picked anyone, that's true. I chose you because I know it's your dream. You once told me you wanted to be there someday and also… I think with you, it'll be the best craic anyway."

Strange how our wishes find their way back to us.

When the festival date finally came and we arrived in Belgium, everything was set. We stayed in a beautiful hotel, surrounded by people from all over Europe who had also won through Coca-Cola. We stepped into the garden and shared our first beer. The heat was fierce, about 33 degrees, and that cold beer tasted like the best thing in the world.

Soon we started chatting with a group of Italians who were also hiding from the sun. We played, sang songs, and the circle under the umbrellas kept growing as more and more people joined. Then suddenly the call for the bus came. Our hotel was about twenty-five minutes from the festival. One of the Coca-Cola guides welcomed us on board.

I was so excited. I still couldn't believe my dream had come true, and that Nick had been the one to make it happen.

On the bus, we met more Dutch people. Nick quickly made friends, one of them named Ivan. At the time, I didn't know it, but Ivan was connected to someone who would change something in my life. He was there with his sister Macy and his wife Yvonne.

The festival itself was breathtaking. The music was loud, people were happy, dancing, smiling, and friendly. It felt like Disneyland for adults, with famous DJs everywhere. The music was like a language everyone understood. People came from all over the world, yet the beats spoke to us all the same.

The ground vibrated with every drop, shaking through my legs as if the festival itself wanted me to dance, even if I didn't want to.

We spent most of the festival as a group, but on the last day it ended up being just Macy and me. Everyone else went their own way. I didn't expect anything, yet sometimes life doesn't wait for expectations.

It happened in a moment, quick and unplanned. A random kiss. No build-up, no signal, just there and somehow, it felt natural. Like the music, the lights, the whole energy of Tomorrowland had pushed us into it.

That little spark changed everything.

We spent the rest of the day together, not caring where the others were. As the daylight faded and the night revealed its beauty, with flashing lights and pounding music, the moment felt even more magical. Macy and I grew closer. We shared a connection, unplanned, simple and real. Those hours became one of the most beautiful memories of that time.

I had no idea where it would lead, the step that would take me into the Netherlands.

On the day I was leaving, my flight from Belgium was very early. Still, I made sure to say goodbye to Macy. We had created something I didn't want to leave without **honouring**. We exchanged numbers. I told her, half-joking that I'd visit if she ever invited me.

She smiled and said, "Yes, you should come for a visit."

Back in Ireland, my mind stayed at the festival, replaying those magical days, still feeling lucky, still amazed at how beautiful it had all been.

A few days later, once life began to settle, I messaged Macy. We started texting, nothing deep, no big conversations about life or meaning just light, funny stories. It was enough to make me smile a lot. Even through the distance, something about her presence reached me.

The Bridge, Not the DestinatiOn

About a month later, I booked a flight to the Netherlands. I was a little nervous. After all, I was flying to visit a woman I had only texted with, and I didn't know what to expect. Still, I had a good feeling.

I flew over for four days. Macy picked me up at the airport. Just like she promised, she brought two little shots for us to take. It was such a beautiful feeling, like I had stepped back into the magic of Tomorrowland.

We had an amazing time together, full of connection and intimacy. She had planned all four days for us, showing me everything she could around the place where she lived.

When we arrived at her house, no words were needed. It felt like we had missed each other for years. It was intense, beautiful, passionate. Time flew. Hours felt like minutes, and days passed too quickly.

It wasn't just about that. We made simple, beautiful memories, cycling to a nearby beach, exploring the city, going to restaurants, tasting food, visiting bars, playing games. Those four days was an amazing. During that time, something shifted in me, as if a weight of past pain cracked and finally broke open.

I didn't know why. Maybe it was because she was so simple, so kind and honest. Maybe it was the way she cared enough to make plans just for us. Small things are what make life spectacular, and after my past they meant so much to me.

Or maybe it was something else… something that told me I was meant to go in this direction, even if I didn't know where it would lead.

On the last night, we were lying beside each other, cuddling in bed. She said, "Look, I don't want anything romantic, but I feel really good in your company… and we also have all this wildness together."

I looked into her eyes and smiled. "So, you don't want me to come back and visit again?"

Her answer came quickly, "Yes, I do want you to come back, but I don't want anything emotional."

We understood each other without needing to say more.

It was September. I left the Netherlands with a full heart and returned to Ireland feeling happy, already thinking about when I'd see Macy again.

For nearly two months, we messaged each other a lot. We laughed and shared stories from each other's lives. Simple, yet it was enough to make me smile. Even through the screen, I felt something.

Then it happened. Slowly, quietly, without permission I started to like Macy more than I should have. My brain kept saying no, reminding me of the distance and the logic. I lived in Ireland; she lived in the Netherlands. It didn't make sense, yet my heart didn't listen. Even when Macy said she didn't want anything romantic, I couldn't help it.

After a very painful relationship in my past, to be with someone good felt like a blessing. I had promised myself not to fall in love again too easily, but it happened. Feelings grew.

It was November, and I had another flight booked to the Netherlands. I felt like a child on Christmas morning, excited and full of energy. I was going for five days this time, and again it was wild and intimate. Macy had made plans again, and it meant so much to me.

For her, maybe it was nothing but for someone like me, someone who had been hurt, manipulated, and nearly lost himself it meant everything. She surprised me with something I had never experienced before; she booked a cinema... but not a normal one. It was a cinema inside a swimming pool. So different. So special.

I thought I was in love then, but when I look back now, I know it wasn't love. It was the way Macy accepted me. She liked me for who I was without trying to change me.

Those five days passed quickly. We made beautiful memories. Before leaving, we planned another visit. I would come again before my birthday in January.

Something shifted inside me after our second meetup. When I came back to Ireland, I felt something I couldn't explain. A pull...a deep gut feeling toward the Netherlands. At the time I thought maybe it was because of Macy.

It was December 2022, I felt something change in her. Slower replies. She started spending a lot of time with a work colleague. One day she said, "My colleague is very upset. I'm going to see him so he's not alone."

I didn't think too much about it.

Then, on the 30th of December, the day before New Year's, I was alone at home in Ireland. My best friend Jozef, who lived with me, was away for the holidays. That's when Macy messaged me saying she needed to talk. I already knew. I felt it before she said it. She told me she was starting to have feelings for her colleague.

I felt crushed, alone. It was as if the past had come back to hit me even harder, reminding me not to build a world only from moments, but to stay in the present. She hadn't lied to me. She told me she didn't want anything romantic. For some reason I couldn't bring myself to tell her that my feelings had changed, because I didn't want to lose her. Instead, I lost myself. Not because of her, but because of me.

My heart wanted to feel, while my eyes helped ignore the truth.

I cried as if the whole world was standing against me. I tried to stay strong, but the pain was stronger. I didn't know who to turn to. So, I called Jozef, the friend who had always been there when I needed him.

After our call, he changed his return flight and came back the next day so I wouldn't be alone. It meant the world to me to have a friend who, no matter what was happening, always had my back when I needed it most.

Yes, I had others too like my mama, my sister, my other close friends but when something like this happens, all you can see is sadness. In those moments, you don't just want someone on the phone, you want someone there with you in the present because once you hang up, the silence returns, and with it, the pain.

I cried for days, maybe a week straight. I kept replaying the memories with Macy in my mind, knowing now they were just that… memories.

Still, something stayed with me. Something deeper than heartbreak.

I started to realise… these feelings I had, this strong pull toward the Netherlands, weren't about Macy. Not really.

At the beginning of January 2023, I started a new job. It came at the perfect time, because I needed something to keep my mind busy, something to distract me from everything that had happened. The job was in the IT department, working remotely from home.

Starting something new, learning new things, kept my mind occupied. I've always been proactive at work, staying late when needed, learning quickly, offering ideas and energy to the project and they saw it. I started getting more responsibilities, I started learning more, I could feel myself growing.

In February, I called my mama. I told her everything about my gut feelings, how I still felt like I needed to go to the Netherlands, even though I couldn't explain why. The feeling was strong. It was more intense, almost like something was pushing me from the inside. I tried not to think much about it, because there was no logic behind it. No clear reason, no clear path.

I stayed in occasional contact with Ivan, Macy's brother, even if we didn't talk often. Macy and I... well, we stopped talking. Not because we weren't friends, but because our lives simply took different directions.

Maybe she was the person I was meant to meet, not to stay in my life forever, but to show me direction. To awaken something in me. To help me unknowingly follow whatever was pulling me toward the Netherlands. To lead me to where I needed to be, for a reason I didn't know.

Two months later, I received an unexpected invitation. It was as if life was gently telling me,

"Go. Move. There's something waiting for you."

Ivan asked me if I'd like to come over for King's Day party. I didn't hesitate. "Yes, of course," I said. Not because of Macy, not out of hope that I'd see her. That chapter had already closed quietly.

There was something deep within me kept whispering... "You're not finished here. This isn't the end. This is just the beginning."

It wasn't just the Netherlands, it was whatever this journey was trying to show me. So, I booked my flight and prepared to go back, and this time not with longing, or hope, or confusion, but with openness.

I didn't know it then, but this trip would change my life completely, or the way I knew life itself, to show me something I could never have understood otherwise.

Not to replace anyone.

Not to erase anything...but, to start... something else.

This was only the beginning.

The Little Things Along the Way

It was April 2023, and I had landed in the Netherlands, with a lighter heart this time. No pressure, no expectations, just curiosity and an unspoken need to be here again.

I didn't know what was calling me so strongly, something I couldn't explain, but I followed the pull, whatever it was trying to show me.

Ivan had given me clear instructions.

"Take the direct train, no transfers needed. Don't worry," he said.

Let's be honest, it wouldn't be me if something unexpected didn't happen.

I had brought two small gifts to thank Ivan and his wife Yvonne for inviting me. A box of chocolates and a special bottle of whiskey. As I got on the train, I felt that familiar nervousness of being somewhere new, not knowing the language. Still, the feeling in my gut was stronger than the fear. I told myself not to stress. Everything would unfold the way it should.

About an hour in, Ivan called to check where I was. I chatted with him while staring out the window. The train stopped at a station. It looked like just another stop, so I didn't pay much attention. Then suddenly, I felt a tap on my shoulder.

A tall man stood beside me. At first, I thought he wanted to see my ticket.

"Sorry, I don't speak Dutch," I said.

He switched to English right away.

"You have to leave this carriage."

Confused, I replied, "No, I'm visiting a friend for the first time, and he told me not to change trains."

The man smiled gently.

"Your carriage has been disconnected from the train. Look."

I turned my head, and there it was, my lovely train, the one I was supposed to stay on, rolling away without me, almost echoing Ivan's words..."Don't change trains."

In my mind I thought, *I didn't expect the train would be the one to change me.*

I just stood there, phone still in my hand, watching it drift off into the distance while I was glued to the half that wasn't going anywhere.

So, I did what I always do. I got off and figured it out.

On the platform, a young girl of maybe fifteen approached me, speaking in Dutch.

"I'm sorry," I said. "I only speak English."

She switched fluently.

"Were you also on the train to Bergen op Zoom?"

"Yes," I said. "Are you going the same direction?"

She looked a little lost. "Do you know when the next train is? Everything's so mixed up."

I told her gently, "Stay here, I'll find out." I went inside the station and asked around. A few people kindly explained which train to take. It was getting dark, so I bought snacks and two bottles of water, then came back. I gave her some food and one of the bottles. Soon the next train arrived.

As I sat down and messaged Ivan to let him know I'd be about an hour late, I suddenly remembered the gift I'd brought for Ivan and Yvonne, the chocolates and whiskey. In the panic, I'd left it behind in the disconnected carriage.

I shook my head. Not frustrated about the gift itself, but because it mattered to me as a gesture. Now it was gone, probably enjoying the journey more than I was.

I laughed to myself.

"Lukas, really? Only you could lose a train and a thank-you in the same day."

On the train, the girl came up to me again.

"Would you mind if I sit here?" she asked. "I don't feel safe near strangers, but you make me feel comfortable."

"Of course," I said.

We had a lovely conversation. She told me about school, where she lived, and her dreams for the future. I shared a few thoughts about life, told her to follow her dreams, to become whatever she truly wanted. She was young, maybe too young to fully understand me, but I believe people should hear it early. Once you believe it, you can build it, maybe even go further than I ever did.

It made me happy to help her, even in a small way.

Eventually, I arrived at my stop. She was continuing on, so I wished her a safe journey. With a smile, I added, half-joking but also serious, "Remember, don't talk to strangers… except maybe the good ones who somehow get disconnected from the train."

She laughed, thanked me for the food and company, and I watched her go, feeling that in a small way I had made her day easier.

It was nearly 10 p.m. when I stepped off the train in Bergen op Zoom. I called Ivan immediately. "I'm finally here."

He came right away. Dinner was waiting. The smells spread through the house like a soft touch of something you'd never tasted but already knew would be good, food that spoke for itself, waiting to be shared. They had prepared everything for me. It didn't feel like I was with people I'd only met once before and spoken to a few times on the phone.

The three of us had a cozy evening. They taught me how to play a board game I'd never seen before. I won.

(Though I still think they let me win.)

Later that night, I lay in bed replaying the day. The disconnected train, the lost gift, the girl I helped, and the board game. I laughed to myself.

What a day, I thought, wondering what tomorrow would bring.

It's funny how accidents, small gestures, and helping someone in need can shape a day.
It's never the grand plans, but the small surprises that turn into the memories we keep and maybe for others too.

At the DoorsteP of SomEthing

Some moments leave more than memories; they carve something new within you.

The next morning, one of Ivan's friends arrived to pick us up for the festival. She was standing at the doorstep.

She looked stunning, her beauty shone from far away. The kind of person you'd notice, the kind of presence that made you turn around once she passed.

She wore a long black dress with a black leather jacket. Simple. Bold. Unforgettable.

Ivan turned to me and said,

"This is Jaya."

I replied softly, "Hi, I'm Lukas."

It was enough for simple conversations. At first, we exchanged only a few words. Once we arrived at the train station, we met more of Ivan's friends and hers. All of us were so excited for the festival. It touched me how kind they were, switching to English whenever they could so I wouldn't feel left out.

Once we arrived at the festival, there were a lot of people waiting in the queue. Music played loudly in the distance. The moment we entered, Jaya suddenly ran over to me, her face lighting up.

"Your energy, OMG!" she said, almost breathless.

I was full of excitement and just wanted to move. I smiled, replied, "I know," and then ran straight into the crowd, disappearing into the music. It was strange the way she said it, but because it was a festival, all I had in my mind was music.

We didn't see each other often during the day.

When the festival ended, we all headed to the bus back to the train station. The evening was cold, and I remember shivering. My legs were sore, barely able to stand after dancing the whole time. All I wanted was to be back home.

As the bus doors opened, we were among the first to get in. I walked over to her and asked,

"Is the seat next to you free?"

She smiled warmly.

"Yes, of course."

We started talking. Her English wasn't perfect and my Dutch was zero yet somehow, it didn't matter. We talked a lot. We laughed even more. Our jokes became our own language. We shared the same sense of humour, and that made time disappear. Somehow, we understood each other without needing all the words.

Something about her felt strange, different from anything I knew before.

Once we arrived at our destination, Ivan told me we were going to his house for a little after-party. Jaya mentioned she had a DJ deck and could play some music. Ivan's father picked us up, but Ivan said only Jaya and I could come which made the evening feel even more unusual.

It was a simple night. A drink, some music, conversations I couldn't follow, but I didn't mind. From time to time, I caught myself glancing at Jaya, careful not to stare.

When it was time for her to leave, she came over, smiled, said it was lovely to meet me, and kissed me gently on the cheek. In that moment, I thought it would be the last time I'd ever see her.

It seems the universe had other plans. At the festival, I had swapped Instagram with a few of Ivan's Dutch friends, Jaya included. The next day, as I packed my suitcase and reflected on all the memories I had made, I flew back to Ireland happy again.

A week later, I sent a funny Dutch video to Ivan's Dutch friends I'd met at the festival. Maybe it wasn't as funny as I thought. Nobody replied.

Except for one person. Jaya.

She didn't just reply with an emoji or reaction. She wrote back to me in English.

We exchanged a few messages that day. Mostly laughing, reminiscing about the party, and remembering the small, funny details from that night. It was simple, yet sometimes, the simplest exchanges are the ones that quietly change the course of everything.

WheN the Universe Opens tHe Door

*I*n the weeks that followed, we began messaging every day. It was unexpected, unlike anything I had ever known before. Our talks grew deeper with each passing day.

It felt as if we had known each other forever, as if there was nothing to fear in opening up. We spoke about everything... our fears, our happiness, our luck, our lives. We discovered so many similarities in our pasts, the strange timing of our meeting, the energy between us. It was uncanny.

Our conversations didn't need a reason. They flowed both ways, like two currents naturally merging.

One day she told me that on the day of the festival, the day we met, she hadn't planned to go. Only the day before, she suddenly felt she had to.

I froze when I heard that.

I told her my story too, how something had been calling me to the Netherlands long before I even knew her.

She taught me things about myself I had never noticed. It was strange; she didn't know me, yet she seemed to know me better than I knew myself.

One day we were talking about health, and I mentioned that I had colitis. To my surprise, she said, "I have colitis too." What shocked us most was that we had both been diagnosed in the same year.

Then came another mirror. We had both been through destructive relationships, the kind that nearly take your soul away. We both ended those relationships in the same year.

We also discovered we had the same eye colour. That alone wasn't unusual. Then came the stranger part... our eyes changed the same way. Greenish in summer. Brownish in winter. That gave us both goosebumps.

The universe seemed to be tapping us on the shoulder, whispering, "Pay attention."

Goosebumps had basically become part of our daily routine. At some point, we started joking.

"Okay... what's next?"

So many of our life experiences mirrored each other. It felt like something far greater than coincidence.

Jaya also began opening up about something new to me. Something I had never really heard before... spirituality. It wasn't part of my world. Not the one I knew. Still, I listened. She shared her personal journey with such honesty that I felt safe enough to open up in return.

One day she asked me,

"Do you know what twin flames are?"

I shook my head.

"No. What does it mean?"

She explained,

"It's an intense soul connection with someone who is considered to be the other half of your own soul. Not everyone has a twin flame. Meeting one is rare, and life-changing."

We even laughed about it, the idea that we might be twin flames, because of all the strange circumstances, the timing, the endless similarities in our lives, and the way we met.

I told her, "Once you have a new relationship, our friendship, our 'twin flame,' will end."

She asked me why I thought that.

I said, "Look, to be honest, I don't think your next one, whoever that might be, would allow this kind of friendship."

She said, "Then I will leave him. I won't let you go, no matter what. I've never experienced something like this before. The connection we share it's strange for me too."

At first, I was in shock. I didn't know if I could believe in twin flames. It sounded too big, too rare, too unreal.

With all the signs between us, the mirrored emotions, the connection, the unspoken understanding, I started to wonder if maybe, just maybe, it was true. What if she was that rare person I was meant to find?

Why else would I feel this way? Why else would I have these strong gut feelings pulling me toward the Netherlands before I even knew her, feelings that made no logical sense?

It wasn't like being in love. Not the usual kind. It was something different. Something deeper. Something you can't explain with words.

Our conversations kept growing, pulling us closer and closer, not just on the surface but deeply.

Around the end of May, just a month after we first met, I told her I had this idea.

I wanted to come back to the Netherlands to study Dutch, if my employer allowed me.

I told her my plan and the lie that came with it. She simply said, "I hope you get approved. I'll pray for you."

My plan was to say that my nanny was sick, and I had to travel to the Netherlands to take care of her for three weeks. I even told my employer she was Dutch, even though she wasn't.

The part I didn't lie about? My feelings.

My nanny had passed away 14 years ago, but the way I described it, the emotion, the loss, it all came from a real place. It was the same grief I had once carried.

Before sending my request, I spoke with my mama about it. I asked her if it was okay to use that story, even if it wasn't nice to do.

She said,

"Lukas, I believe your nanny would want to help you. I know she's still with you, even now, after all these years."

My feeling about going to the Netherlands, even for a short time, was so strong. I would do what I could just to find out why.

I was able to arrange accommodation in Leiden, where I planned to study Dutch, almost as if I already knew I would get the approval. That was my official plan for three weeks, but truthfully, I was also hoping to see her.

It was June 2023, I sent the request to my general manager and waited, hoping for the best.

The next day, I got a call. My stomach was doing flips, like I was on a rollercoaster.

The voice said,

"Lukas, I don't know how you did it, but you impressed the general manager with the way you work. You've been approved. Not just for three weeks, but for three and a half months. But you have to leave in two weeks."

I didn't know whether to laugh or panic. Somehow, I'd been approved to work from abroad. Out of all the employees, I was the only one.

At the same time, I thought, *Oh no!*

I had a three-week place booked, starting four weeks from now. Now I had to leave in two and stay for three and a half months.

A wave of fear and excitement hit me at once, sharp enough to twist my stomach, bright enough to make me smile.

I messaged Jaya right away. She was so happy for me.

I also told her my concern,

"I don't have a place to stay for that long. I wasn't expecting this. I thought I'd be there just a few weeks."

Then, out of nowhere, she surprised me.

She said, "I know this might sound crazy, but come and live in my house. I trust you."

She also told me, "I've never invited a man to my house before. I have two kids, and when they're with me, no man ever stays over."

I said, "This is crazy."

We both started laughing, underneath it all deep down, we were both happy.

We trusted each other, even though we had only known each other through messages.

It felt right. It felt safe.

We promised each other this would be the best summer of our lives. That we'd enjoy it together.

Then she asked, "How are you going to study?"

I completely froze.

I had forgotten, my Dutch course wasn't online. It was in the classroom.

The only thing I could think to do was send an email to the university and ask if it was possible to switch online because of personal circumstances.

The next day they replied,

"Hi Lukas, your course has been changed from in-class to online due to lecture capacity."

I shared the message with Jaya, and we were both speechless.

We couldn't find the words to describe how perfectly everything was falling into place.

This no longer felt like coincidence. It was more than luck.

Move to the Netherlands. Meet Jaya. Meet my twin flame.

Something deep inside me was already guiding me toward her. Now, the pieces were starting to make sense.

I began to believe in something more than just an ordinary life. It was something else.

I started preparing everything. I was the happiest man in the world.

Increasingly, I believed that what was pulling me to the Netherlands wasn't just a gut feeling. It was real.

I started to like Jaya more and more, as if she were my destiny.

I didn't want to risk the connection we had, not by saying too much, not too soon.

A week before my flight, Jaya went to Budapest with a friend.

They had a great time, and even while she was there, we kept texting. She shared everything with me, her stories, her moments, even photos of where she was and who she was with.

One morning I woke up to a missed WhatsApp call from her at 2 a.m.

I messaged her,

"Come on, tell me the story. Why did you call me at 2 in the morning?"

She admitted she'd been drunk, uncomfortable, and followed by a strange guy. That's why she tried to call me, but when I didn't answer, she added something that twisted my stomach... "I called my ex, Roko."

I already knew about him, manipulative, dark, the kind of person you don't want back in your life.

I laughed nervously,

"Yep, that was stupid."

On the inside, I was afraid, afraid she might go back to him.

Not long after, she messaged me,

"Lukas, I feel like you have different feelings for me than I have for you. I just want to say I value our connection, and I don't want to lose what we have."

I answered honestly,

"Yes, I do like you more than other women I've known, but I also value our connection, and I can keep it at a friendship level."

Of course I could, but with everything she had told me, the way she always messaged me, the promises we made, I was confused.

The last two days of her stay in Budapest, she changed.

Fewer messages. Shorter replies.

After that call with her ex, something shifted.

I had booked my flight to Amsterdam for the same day she was returning from Budapest, so she and her friend could pick me up.

When I saw her, I froze. I couldn't believe I was seeing her again. It felt like a dream. Like all the signs I had received were for this moment.

From the airport, we headed to the car park, looking for their car.

It was so small. I laughed and said,

"Are you sure I'll even fit in here?"

We barely managed to squeeze in all the suitcases, including me.

On the way, I realised something. She didn't speak much English. It hit me. All those messages we exchanged, all those deep conversations… she had probably used Google Translate often.

It made me realise just how much effort she put in, just to talk to me. That meant something. Something no one else had ever done for me.

When we arrived at her friend's house, her friend got out of the car, passed the key to Jaya, took her suitcase and said,

"Okay, I'm home. Enjoy the rest of the trip."

Suddenly, it was just the two of us. No friends. No distractions. For the first time.

I was a little nervous but also happy. Once we got into her hometown, she parked in a small car park in a lovely area, with cute little houses lined up next to each other. I already felt good there.

We took our suitcases and started walking toward the houses. They all looked the same.

Then she smiled and said,

"Okay, since we have so many similarities and can feel each other's energy... try to guess which house is mine."

To me, they all looked identical. Without hesitation, I started walking down the narrow street, trying to feel which one could be hers.

She laughed and called out,

"Lukas! You didn't get this one right."

She opened the door. From the outside, the house didn't look like anything special.

That all changed the moment I stepped inside, it was beautiful. She showed me around and then took me upstairs to see my room. It was on the second floor with a large bed. It felt good, but still strange.

As soon as we dropped our bags, she turned to me and said,

"Okay, what are we going to do? Let's go party!"

I wasn't against it.

"Let's go dance," I said.

It was around 10 p.m. She disappeared upstairs to change. I joked, "Don't take forever."

When she came down, my words caught in my throat.

A red dress. Tight, beautiful. It seemed to steal the light from the hallway.

She smiled, a little shyly.

"What do you think?"

I paused, breath stuck in my chest. Finally, all I managed was, "Wow."

I wanted to say more, but nothing came.

We drove into Breda to meet her friend, the streets alive with music and people spilling out of clubs...but I only saw her, the girl in the red dress.

Inside the club, the heat wrapped around us, the air thick with bass. I went straight to the bar and ordered three apple juices with ice, but the whole room had already turned to look at her. She laughed, hair falling over her shoulder, and for a moment I forgot to breathe.

We danced, but I needed space, so I slipped outside. A minute later she followed, found me across the street. She stopped to talk to someone she knew in Dutch.

When she turned back, her hand found mine.

"I don't feel good. Can we go home?"

I laughed with relief.

"That's exactly what I was thinking. I didn't want to ruin your night."

We left her friend behind and drove through the quiet streets, windows open, laughter spilling into the night.

Honestly, the best part of that night wasn't the party at all. It was the headlights on empty roads, her laughter beside me. It felt like the beginning of everything we had promised each other. Our very first memory, just the two of us.

The PromisE and the Shadow

The days that followed felt like the promise we once made in messages, that this summer would be the best one for us. We laughed. We travelled. We talked late into the night. Nothing between us felt heavy. Nothing boring.

One evening we chose a movie. I asked if it would bother her to scratch my head. She smiled, set a pillow on her legs, and said, "Don't get used to it."

When the screen went dark, we talked about life. Our eyes met, slow and unexpected, the kind of moment where the air forgets how to move. Music played softly. I thought of kissing her, but I didn't. Maybe I was afraid I was the only one who felt it. After this, something shifted, like a step back in her.

The next day our words grew fewer. She stayed longer in her room, her phone always in her hand. She said she was going to a party Friday coming with her friend, I asked if I could come. She said no.

Two days later before the weekend hit I couldn't hold it in.

"Do you want to talk? I feel like something changed."

"No, I don't want to," she answered.

"Hey, come on. Whatever it is, we can talk it out," I said, using one of our old jokes just to break the silence.

"It feels like you're starting to have feelings for me more than you should. We agreed to keep boundaries."

"I promised I wouldn't cross that line," I told her. "If I did something wrong, tell me and I won't do it again."

The tension lifted. We laughed. She said she had wanted to invite her friend, but after the movie night it didn't feel right. "Now that I know everything is okay between us, we can have a house party instead."

Friday came. Her friend arrived after work.

"This is Inga," she said, "and this is Lukas."

It didn't take long before we were chatting like a radio show, like friends who had known each other for years.

We had our first drinks when Jaya said, "There's something I need to tell you. You're the two people I trust most. I also invited my ex-boyfriend, Roko."

Silence. I thought of the stories I'd heard, none of them kind. Suddenly all the hours she spent on her phone made sense. It reminded me of Ireland, when our phones did the talking for us. The illusion I'd been holding cracked.

Later, we sat in the garden. Really, it was just Inga and I talking while Jaya stared at her screen. Then he arrived. Roko. A shadow seemed to walk with him. Darkness followed wherever he stepped kind of feelings.

When Jaya introduced us, I tried some humour.

"Where have you been so long? We've been waiting and couldn't start drinking without you."

No answer. He sat beside Jaya. She smiled, glowing like a child with a new toy and I disappeared from the picture.

He talked a lot, but not in a language I could understand. Inga noticed. When he spoke in Dutch to her, she replied in English. At one point she said, "Why don't you speak English? Lukas can't understand," and winked at me. That night, Inga became my unexpected ally.

Still, the air was split. Them and us. Inga and I often left his company, and I think Jaya started to notice. She tried to join us, but every time he came, Inga and I moved somewhere else.

When he left for the bathroom, Jaya asked, "So … what do you think?"

"His vibe is cold, you can sense the bad vibes" we both said.

She nodded. "Yes. I feel it too, but what do we do? He wants to stay over."

We laughed. "That's your business, not ours."

Three of us came up with a plan. It was simple. Pretend to go to bed, leave her to do the talking. Minutes later she told him he couldn't stay. His look as he left was sharp and unsettling.

She walked him to the door and, once he left, closed it hard. Then she ran to me, jumped into my arms, and kissed me softly. Not like in movies. Short and unexpected, but enough to wake every thought I'd held back.

That night she curled into me on the garden couch. Inga covered us with a blanket. We talked under the stars. Jaya never let me go.

For a moment, life felt whole again.

The days after blurred into happiness. Inga stayed longer. We laughed, we planned Awakenings Festival, and before she left, she promised to meet us there.

The morning of the festival carried its own electricity. Over breakfast we imagined the night ahead.

When we arrived, the air was alive. Music thumped through the fields, sun poured over the crowds. We joined a group of her friends, Ivan and his wife Yvonne among them, the only two faces I already knew. We took lots of photos and videos so the memory would never vanish from our minds.

The day unfolded perfectly at first. Jaya and I danced, had a few drinks, laughed, and shared each other's food. The music, the people, the light, it all felt like it belonged. Like a dream you once had walking into daylight.

At one point she grabbed my hand and whispered, "Come with me," pulling me through the crowd.

On the path to another stage, she met a man. They started talking while I tried to let the music hold me. She leaned close to him, and I felt myself fading, like the song no longer reached my ears. In that moment I realised how quickly closeness can turn into distance. Then she turned.

"Go with the others. I'll go with him."

The crowd kept cheering. I felt quiet.

Just like that, she was gone.

Darkness had fallen. I searched for the group but couldn't find them. I messaged Inga so we could meet, because I'd lost everyone.

"Where's Jaya?" she asked.

"She left with some guy."

Her face said everything. She messaged Jaya, but no reply came. I spent the night with Inga and her boyfriend, trying to lose myself in the music.

Near the end, a message arrived from Jaya... *Where are you?* It felt cold, like a door slamming shut. I told her I was with Inga. She told me to come back.

When I did, she barely looked at me, barely spoke. Or maybe it was just me, overthinking what had happened. Back at the house, everything was different. Words turned short. Laughter disappeared. It was like she felt angry at me, and I didn't know why. She said she was tired and went to bed. At night, I could hear her voice, soft and fast in Dutch, through the walls.

It hurt. I replayed the festival in my head, searching for the mistake. My mind circled back to me, to what I must have done wrong.

That was my habit. My ex had trained me well. She told me often enough that things were my fault, and somewhere deep inside, I believed her. I had healed most of it, but a piece still clung like a shadow I didn't know how to throw away. Overthinking, blame became mine.

So, I lay there again, wondering what I had done wrong, when maybe the truth was simple. It was never about me at all. It was about her world, her shadows, and me learning not to carry them as my own.

From WArmth to Winter

Another week passed and her kids were coming over again. One day, Jaya told me her dad would stay because she was going out with a friend. He would babysit with me. I didn't mind, but I wasn't sure how he'd see me, a stranger in his daughter's home.

He was kind, full of stories, many of which were funny. After Jaya put the kids to sleep, she left, and her dad and I talked for a while. He told me about moving to the Netherlands and about other parts of his life. We got on well. After a while, he said he was tired and went to sleep. As he was staying in the room that I had been using most of the time, I slept on the couch again that night.

That night, I woke to a child's cry. Instinct took over. I ran upstairs with my phone light. Her dad was snoring a floor above, but I didn't think to wake him. In the room, I found her daughter crying for her mama, speaking Dutch. The only word I caught was "mama."

I opened Google Translate, trying to record what she said. She was asking where her mama was and wondering when she would be back. She said that she was scared and didn't want to be alone. I typed a reply and let the app tell her that her mama would be back soon and she didn't need to worry.

As I stepped away, she held my hand and said something else in Dutch. Again, I used Translate. She was asking if I could stay with her because she was afraid of the dark. She always slept beside her mama.

I said okay. I typed it into Translate so she could hear and understand. I pulled the blanket over her and lay down beside her, planning to wait until she fell asleep and leave. I didn't expect how tightly she would hold my hand. It felt like she was my own child. A warm, protective feeling I had never known before.

I messaged Jaya to let her know what happened and told her that if she came home and found me there, I had probably fallen asleep.

Hours later, phone light on my face woke me. It was Jaya, smiling as she took a picture of me and her daughter.

"What are you doing?" I asked.

"You two looked so cute," she said, still smiling.

She thanked me for helping while she was away, and I went back downstairs to the couch.

After that night, her daughter always came to me. On walks, she held my hand. When the four of us played games, she chose me. I think Jaya noticed. She hadn't expected her kids to grow so attached so quickly.

After the kids left, something changed. Jaya began spending most evenings on the phone, talking more about her ex-boyfriend. Once she even asked what I thought. I told her honestly,

"You're falling into his game again. He knows you well, and he knows how to play you."

She resisted.

"No, I've changed. Now I'm the one playing the game. He's scared to lose me again. He doesn't know me like this. I'm much stronger."

I saw it differently. The more I tried to explain, the more distant we became. I stopped mentioning it, but I could feel they were back in touch. In that moment I started to think… why does she even want to be with him. This doesn't sound like love. Instead of happiness, it felt like anger.

Our conversations grew fewer. She had other plans. One day she came home and said, half annoyed,

"Oh, you're here again."

I hadn't realised how much time I spent in the living room. I didn't know where else to be. Sometimes I walked the city, but I had no routine, no hobbies there yet. Her home was her peace, her safe space. Now I was always there.

That Friday, after she dropped the kids to her ex-husband, she said she was going out with a friend. No details. Around 2:40 a.m. I woke and went downstairs to watch a movie. By coincidence, Jaya came home ten minutes later.

Seeing me there, she asked sharply, "Oh, you're here again. Did you wait for me?"

I explained I had just woken and couldn't sleep, that it was a coincidence. She didn't answer. She went straight to her room.

The next morning before work, I asked if we could talk, because I felt something was wrong. She didn't reply. She just closed the door hard behind her.

I started blaming myself. Maybe I was too much. Too present. Old insecurities flooded back.

That evening she came home with her friend Inga.

"Do you want to talk?" she asked.

"Yes," I said, relieved.

"I want you to leave. Now!"

Cold sweat ran through me. "Can we talk about it? I don't understand what happened. If I did something wrong, I'm sorry."

She stood and walked into the garden, like I wasn't there.

Her friend Inga came over to me instead.

"Lukas, it wasn't right that you didn't wake Jaya's father the other night when her daughter cried... it's strange, you're still a stranger here."

I explained I hadn't thought, I simply reacted. I heard a child crying and acted. Jaya knew me, I never thought it was wrong. Only later I realised that others might see it differently, that maybe waking the dad would have been expected, a parent's role, a cultural boundary, but in that moment, instinct was all I followed.

I said I needed a short walk to breathe and think, then I would come back to pack.

Outside, tears came with the anger. My gut was tight. I felt sick. Blaming myself, I wondered why I trusted so much again. My positive energy was gone; sadness and blame took over my mind. I couldn't go back to Ireland...my employer had said I couldn't return early. I worried I'd lose my job. I had no place to live. Everything I built vanished in the click of a finger. How would I even get to work tomorrow if I didn't have a place to stay?

I checked online. Rooms were rare. Whole apartments asked for huge deposits and full rent upfront, money I didn't have. Some wanted €3,000 before even moving in. Hotels were €150–200 per night, which would burn through my saving quickly.

It was the darkest moment of my life so far. I couldn't tell my mom. I didn't want her to worry.

I tried an old high school friend, but he was in Denmark. He gave me the number of someone else we both knew; someone I hadn't spoken to in almost twenty years. I sent a message. No reply.

I called Ivan.

"Can I stay with you? Jaya doesn't want me here anymore. She told me to leave today."

"Okay, Lukas," he said. "But only for two nights. We're friends, but I have my life with my wife. I don't want this to affect our friendship."

I understood. I was thankful even for that little help. He'd collect me later. I had no idea what would happen after those two nights.

Back at the house, I packed. June to July, that's all it took to turn everything upside down. Why did she change? What happened to the person I trusted, the one I told my fears and dreams to? The person who once lifted me up now threw me out like rubbish.

She avoided me completely. Her friend only said, "Good luck."

I walked out with my head down. Behind me I heard laughter before the door closed. The flash of memory flowed through my mind. I had lived this situation before, but on the other side where the laugh came from. I was empty. Angry. Questioning everything. Was it all in my head? Was the connection even real? My mind mocked me. My heart said something else… don't give up. This isn't the end. Life is showing you something you can't yet see.

Ivan picked me up. He spoke with Jaya in Dutch. It didn't sound friendly.

"Only two nights," he reminded me.

"I know," I said.

That evening, around 9 p.m., my phone rang. It was the schoolmate I had messaged earlier. We hadn't spoken in nearly 20 years. "Hey, how are you? I know it's been years, but… I was wondering if you could help me."

We talked. He said yes, I could stay.

"But you'll need to pay rent upfront. Send me the money now so I know you're serious."

I agreed and sent it. Relief dropped through me like a stone. A way out.

He could collect me after work, around 1 a.m. Two days later, he arrived. He lived thirty minutes from Utrecht and two and a half hours from where he collected me. The apartment was under reconstruction, the roof damaged, so I stayed in the living room. I didn't care. I was grateful.

A little magic had found me again. A reminder that something, God or the universe, was still watching.

While lying on that couch, I couldn't stop thinking about Jaya. The laughter. The stories. The synchronicities. The closeness. How quickly it vanished, the same way it began. At the time, I thought it was just heartbreak. Later I understood it differently.

When I first heard "twin flame," I thought it meant perfect love, two souls united forever. That's how people write about it. With time, I learned it was something else for me.

Jaya used to talk about awakenings. I nodded, smiled, pretended I understood. I didn't. Not until after we separated. Not until Utrecht, broken but strangely aware, beginning to see the world differently.

Twin flames don't just show you love. They show you a mirror, and in it, the parts you tried to bury. Old fears. Old wounds. Hidden shadows. They don't come to break you. They come to crack you, to wake you.

That's what Jaya did. She didn't just make me feel seen at the beginning. She drew the light inside me out, not with anger but with peace, to face myself. It wasn't easy to understand it. It wasn't soft. It was deep. Painful. Transforming.

I later read that twin flames often go through separation. Time apart gives space to grow, to find yourself. Sometimes, it even prepares the way to come back stronger.

It isn't about fighting. It's about becoming.

Maybe, without knowing it, Jaya had helped me take the first step. I didn't know where the road would lead, only that something inside me had already begun to change.

A New Language, A New PaRt of Me

Me and my friend Stefan, the one I started living with in Soest, were talking about so many things, catching up on nearly twenty years we'd missed.

We shared stories about everything we'd gone through since high school, and slowly we became close again. Actually, even closer than before, better friends than we ever were when we just knew each other from the town we once lived in.

I hadn't realised he was spiritual too. It was a surprise, but a good one. Our conversations weren't just about life events anymore. We talked about meaning, the universe, signs, energy.

I kept asking myself where all these people were coming from. I never noticed them before. Now it felt like everyone I met was open, spiritual. Maybe I wasn't ready for those conversations before. or maybe the people around me weren't.

I used to think it was rare to meet someone real, truthful and connected but you can always feel the difference. Some people say they're spiritual, but when it's not real, you just know.

I listened a lot. Stefan often asked me questions because, as he said, "You always give answers I never thought about before." I listened to his struggles, his pain, and I tried to give him a different point of view. Maybe he couldn't see it because he was stuck in a circle he couldn't get out of.

While these talks opened me up in one way, the Dutch course began to open me up in another.

At the same time, I had started my Dutch course through Leiden University. I remember my first introduction class clearly. There were fifteen of us. The lecturer went around asking how long each person had been living in the Netherlands, because the course wouldn't be in English, everything would be taught in Dutch. Some people said two years. Some said four. One said a year and a half. Then she asked me.

"And you, Lukas?"

I smiled. "Three and a half weeks."

She looked surprised. "Why did you sign up for such an intense course if you've only been here a short time?"

I told her the truth. I came here to study Dutch, to push myself, to practice what I'd already been learning with Duolingo, but deep down I knew the real reason. I wanted to understand one person. The person who once was so close to me but now was gone. I kept that to myself and only answered with a smile.

I hadn't given up on the language just because things with Jaya hadn't worked out. In fact, I started to believe maybe this was how it was meant to be, to prove to myself I could do it. Even if it wasn't easy, I don't give up on things at the snap of a finger.

I was working full-time and studying five hours a day, five days a week. It felt like being back in college. Studying a language I had barely heard before was harder than I expected, more than I thought I could manage.

Now I know, if I had still been living with Jaya, my attention would be somewhere else. I would've been too focused on us, and not on what I had signed up for.

We went through twenty-four pages of the Dutch book every single day, for twenty-three days in a row. When the weekend came, it felt like Christmas. Stefan helped me a lot, explaining Dutch in ways I could understand, especially because we spoke the same native language. It made all the difference.

The questions started popping up in my mind again. Why did all this happen? Was there a reason I couldn't see yet? Something written in the stars? Destiny? It didn't make much sense at the time, but I could feel the edges of the puzzle starting to appear.

After weeks of studying, the final exam came. I had to pass listening, writing, and speaking. I was nervous. I didn't sleep the night before, that was always my way before exams. The last two days I lived inside that Dutch book. Stefan supported me every second. He taught me. He pushed me.

The minimum score to pass was 80%. When the results came, I got 85%. I couldn't believe it. I was so proud of myself.

That day when Stefan came back from work, I told him the news. He looked at me and said, "Lukas... you came to the Netherlands to study Dutch. You've only been here a few weeks, you worked full-time, and now you have an A1 certificate from Leiden University. Some people are here five years and still don't speak this much Dutch. I don't know anyone like you. You didn't give up, even after everything."

When I heard those words, I started to cry. It wasn't because of what he said, it was because something inside me finally answered. For the first time I felt it deep within myself, that I was strong, that I didn't give up, that I didn't need anyone else to say, "I'm proud of you." Because this time I heard it from me. That changed everything.

I asked myself if this was another moment meant to change me. Something that shifted me quietly into becoming something more?

The person who started to believe in himself again, after being told otherwise in the past.

It felt like life wasn't about proving I was good enough anymore, but about truly understanding what it meant to live. To grow, to let go, and to rise, not for anyone else but for myself. To see who I was inside… a fighter who can't be broken, even when the odds are stacked against me.

I started questioning… was this how it was supposed to happen? Was Jaya part of it, to push me out, to nearly make me lose my job, to make me feel what it means to lose almost everything and still not give up? Was I meant to reconnect with a friend I hadn't spoken to in nearly twenty years, to pass Dutch, just so I could start seeing myself again and find the strength I thought was gone? Was this just coincidence, or the beginning of something else? In that little moment it wasn't anger but a kind of peace that reminded me…

I rise because I finally see the strength within me.

The Middle of Nowhere, and Every Thing

I was trying to forget Jaya, not the connection, not what I'd learned, but her as a person. If I ever wanted to move on, I had to find a way to separate the past from the present. Somehow, she always found her way back into my thoughts. Almost like the universe didn't want me to forget, only to understand.

A few weeks into living with Stefan, I had a tattoo appointment in Belgium. I'd booked it back when I was still staying with Jaya. We had planned to go together, she was supposed to drive me there. The studio was in a small village, far from everything, and I hadn't realised how complicated it would be to get there from where I'd moved. All I knew was that if I missed my last train home, I'd be stranded. I could easily cancel the appointment, but still, I went.

Antwerp station was enormous. "How am I supposed to get from here to some tiny dot on the map?" I thought. People helped me figure it out, pointing me toward the right train, giving me times. Each kindness felt like a small light guiding me forward. When I finally got off at the last station, there was almost nothing. Just one small building, silence and emptiness all around. It felt like the edge of the world, like those old Texas movies where even the wind had a voice. There were a few people waiting, and I asked how to get to the place. Someone said a bus would come.

It was delayed, and by then I was already worrying I'd miss my appointment. When the bus finally arrived, I told the driver where I needed to go, if there was any stop nearby. He smiled, said he knew the place, and offered to stop near the studio even though there wasn't a real stop there. By the time I reached the studio, I already felt the day turning into something unusual. I greeted them with my little "Hoi, goedenavond!", a scrap from Duolingo. They laughed kindly, the way people do when they see you trying. It made me feel welcome, less like a stranger in the middle of nowhere.

Jullie, the tattoo artist, asked me to wait half an hour. I didn't mind. I'd already learned this day was about patience. While waiting, I talked with the studio receptionist, and soon a friend of his joined us from the restaurant across the street. He brought me an Irish coffee, free of charge. "Just a little gift from the middle of nowhere," he said. It was such a simple thing, yet it felt like the universe was reminding me...*You're not alone.*

When Jullie returned, we looked at the design together. She suggested a few changes that made it even better. Before starting, we stepped outside for a cigarette, and that's when she asked, "Where's Jaya?" I kept it polite, told her Jaya was busy and that I'd moved for my studies to a different city. She didn't need to know more.

The session lasted about four hours, and in those hours the conversation opened something in me. Jullie had this calm presence, almost like an old soul wrapped in quiet energy, and the way she spoke gave me a different point of view. We talked about life, about stories, about loss and beginnings. At one point she recommended a book, and I laughed, telling her the last book I read was probably a case study in college and that I wasn't much of a reader. There was something in the way she said it made me promise I'd give it a try.

She went on to speak about twin flames and awakenings, about seeing life differently. She never pushed, but she did open doors with her words. Before we finished, she said "You should write every day, keep a little diary so you know what's happening in your life, because we usually don't notice the little things. To see what's happening in your life or around you." In my head I thought, *Sure, maybe,* but her words disappeared in my mind before they could settle in.

When it was over, I asked where the train station was and how far. "It's far. You'd never find it on your own. I'll drive you." Relief washed over me. Her kindness wasn't loud, but it stayed with me. That night, I caught each train by minutes, arriving back in Soest just after midnight. Exhausted, with a new tattoo on my skin, a strange book on its way to my door, and a quiet sense of peace I hadn't felt in a long time.

I realised it wasn't just about the ink. It was about the journey, about the strangers who became helpers, the artist who became a guide, the reminder that even in the middle of nowhere, life can place exactly the people you need on your path. It felt like a pause, like the universe had given me one gentle night of calm before sending me back into the storm.

For the first time, I wasn't rushing ahead. I was here.

The Right Time

⁙

*J*aya didn't vanish in days or weeks from my mind. While I was trying to enjoy life, going out on my own, discovering new places, meeting new people and making new friends. I had my little book from Jullie's suggestion with me most of the time. It had started to interest me, almost like my own dictionary of the Netherlands. I could feel something shifting inside me from painful to peaceful.

I remember one day in Utrecht. I went on my own, just me and the book. I found a nice restaurant, sat down, ordered food and a small pint of beer. While reading, I felt different. Relaxed. Grounded. I had always been the kind of person who had people around. Now presence was different. I could hear people talking, birds singing, the noise of the streets. Somehow, I had started living in the present without even realising how.

Before I moved to the Netherlands, I had heard that one of my old friends, Itta, someone I had not spoken to in nearly seven years, had ended her relationship, not by her choice. Even though we had not spoken for so long, I felt bad for her because I knew how hard it probably was. To love someone deeply and then one day, have it all gone.

I messaged her, *I'm sorry for what happened. I hope you're doing okay. If you ever want to talk, give me a call or drop a message.*

A few months later, while I was in the Netherlands, she finally replied. After that came our first call in seven years. We were both in bits, destroyed by what had happened, Itta with her life, me with mine. She was alone in Australia. I was alone in the Netherlands. I don't know why her reply came so late, but it came at the right time.

Maybe that is why we could support each other. We listened to each other's stories. When tears started falling, and they often did, we held each other back from drowning in them. Our friendship became stronger than before, maybe because we were alone, and to have someone to talk to openly, without shame, was something we both needed at the time.

Maybe the universe wanted us to share each other's heaviness. To help each other get through it.

The conversations helped us both. Seeing our situations from different points of view, we could show each other the brighter side of it all. Strange how sometimes life throws a friend back at you just when you need them the most.

Conversations with Itta helped me understand something deeply. I needed to let go, no matter how strong the connection between me and Jaya was. To let good and bad show their true faces. Not to keep one and hide the other.

I think we both helped each other to stop holding on to the bad things so tightly in our minds. I finally understood that Jaya had already given me something no one else ever could. She had given me my life back.

To see the truth and not let anger take control, but to try to understand the anger and walk hand in hand with both good and bad. That realisation brought me peace. Quietly, I asked myself...*Was everything in my life leading me here to finally understand myself?*

One week before I was supposed to return to Ireland, I got a call from my boss. She asked if I would like to extend my stay for another month, "to spend more time with family," she said, since I had finally told them my nanny had passed.

I could not lie anymore to my manager, she had been too good to me. Too supportive.

In my head, I thought my time in the Netherlands had come to an end. Deep inside, I felt something else. Or maybe it was another sign? A whisper from the universe asking, *are you sure you are ready to leave?*

Why would I stay longer? What reason would there be?

No. I knew why I had come here. To be with Jaya. To change. To learn about myself. To meet people who guided me. To follow the signs. To face myself. To let go of ego.

To begin truly awakening to life and the present.

To learn so much about myself.

To see the unseen.

It had all happened for a reason. Or maybe it was just the beginning. A sign of something still waiting ahead, something I could not predict.

For once, I was ready for whatever came next. Strong in heart, wiser in mind, looking for truth, not the illusions I had always created.

The Call That Set Me Free

Three and half months pass very quickly and the day of my return to Ireland came.

It felt different, like I was leaving the place where I was born… or the place I lived for so many years because in this short period of time I learn about myself more than ever.

I sat alone at the airport, thinking about how it was when I first arrived. Someone had been waiting for me. Now, no one was.

It felt like sadness wanted to pull me down, but then my thoughts shifted. I started to remember the funny moments, the things I had learned, the beautiful people I had met. People who guided me, like Jullie or Jaya who didn't break me just crack me to open. This time it wasn't anger that I remembered. It was the things she changed in me when she pushed me out from her house.

I smiled because I realised, I wasn't alone. Not here. Not in this airport. I was standing with a stronger version of myself. The man who had come to the Netherlands didn't see the world the way I see now, but he had the same eyes. That realisation made me smile again.

It showed me how much I had changed and my heart? … instead of closing open more.

In September when I arrived back in Ireland, back home to Clonmel, the first person who obviously couldn't wait to see me was one of my best friends, Jozef, with a million questions. We talked for hours, laughing most of the time. At the end of the night, he looked at me and said, "Lukas… you've changed. I can't explain it… but you are not the same person as you were before. You're still the same you, but something in you is different. In a good way."

I smiled because I knew what he meant. I felt it, too. I was awake. Or at least on the path of awakening.

Life resumed. Same job. Same people. Same streets. Yet everything inside me felt different. It was hard to explain. I started seeing people for who they truly were, from the inside out.

One night at *The Baker*, a girl tried to pull me into the old life by flirting, asking me to kiss her, even inviting me home. A year ago, I might have said yes. This time, I didn't. Not because she wasn't beautiful, but because I knew my worth. I wasn't looking for a night. I had started to believe in true love again, just like before my ex took that away from me. After that experience, I stopped going out as much. Not because I didn't want to, but because it no longer interested me. I began searching for something else. Something quieter. Something real.

I didn't quit going out completely. Maybe once every couple of months, to have a dance, meet some friends. Even then, I preferred meeting them for dinner, going to the cinema, or just sitting and talking. Drinking lost its appeal. It wasn't healthy for me anyway. It just didn't feel like me anymore.

I began to see value elsewhere. I wanted to talk about life. I wanted to meet people who could teach me something I didn't know. I liked meaningful conversations, to hear people's stories, to understand what shaped them. I wanted deep, open conversations, the kind most people are afraid to have because they worry others might call them crazy or miss understood. Those were the only conversations that ever felt true.

Near the end of September, I was driving home from the gym. I had started working on myself again, not to impress anyone, but because I wanted to feel good in my own skin. It was about respect, one small step at a time. That's when my phone rang, I couldn't believe the name on the screen. It was Jaya. After nearly four months of silence.

I picked up not with anger but with peace and said, "Hi... what a surprise. How are you?"

She smiled, I heard it in her voice, and so did I. I wasn't angry with her. I was just happy to hear her voice.

We talked for almost three hours. We had never called each other before, only messages. She asked, "Are you still in the Netherlands?"

I told her, "No, I came back three weeks ago. Why do you ask?"

She said, "I'm so sorry for what I did to you. I listened to others, even though I knew who you really are, deep inside. It's been bothering me. That was supposed to be our best summer... do you remember? We promised that to each other, and I messed it up, with the one person I trusted the most."

In that moment, I remembered the call I got back when I was in the Netherlands, the one asking if I wanted to stay for one more month. Had I ignored the sign? Had I let my analytical mind win again?

I didn't know for sure, but I made myself a quiet promise right then, the next time, I wouldn't ignore the signs. Even if they make no sense. Even if no one else understood, because sometimes it's not logic that leads you...it's knowing.

I told her not to worry. Her words meant a lot to me because I knew I hadn't done anything wrong, but I didn't need confirmation from others to know that too. I had done everything I could to make things okay. To heard it felt good, like a stone fell from my heart, one that had been quietly drowning me for so long.

I wasn't crazy, I didn't need to blame myself anymore.

We spoke like we did before, two people who trusted each other. She told me her kids were sad after I left. Especially her older daughter. They were confused. They kept asking about me even though I had only been there for three weeks.

She kept apologising, but I told her, "It's okay. You didn't do anything wrong. You acted how you felt in the moment. The choice was yours. I'm not angry. You showed me things about myself I never knew. You showed me a kind of life no one else ever could".

She said she missed our connection, but I was already somewhere else. Knew my worth.

I told her maybe one day we meet again, who knows.

Before she hung up, she said something unexpected, "Lukas... I must block you now, because of everything that has happened between us." She had started seeing Roko again, and maybe she didn't want to be reminded of me, of us.

I simply replied, it's okay. Do whatever you feel is best for you. Those were our last words. Then, just like that, she blocked me.

I wasn't angry, I found peace because I knew it wasn't really about me. I understood that we all have our own paths, and sometimes we need to walk them alone to grow. To understand.

That evening, I went to bed with a lot of thoughts. I was happy that she called me and spoke with me. I think it takes courage and a lot of care to call someone and apologise after what's happened. There was something else beyond an ordinary connection between us. She didn't say it out loud, but her call showed she cared about me deeply or was the guilt what's happened.

Meeting Jaya taught me more than I ever thought possible. Things I wouldn't have learned without her. Was it love, what I felt for her? Was the twin flame that should healed me? I kept asking myself.

I knew what love meant. I had felt it before however this was different because for the first time, I understood what it means to love unconditionally, to love without expecting anything in return.

It was understanding. It was the feeling of connection not just surface touch something I never experienced before.

That night, I lit a candle, like I always do before bed, but this time I wasn't just remembering the past anymore. I was thanking it slowly, letting go of it, and honouring what it taught me.

To love is to open yourself without guarantees, but hiding your heart forever is the only choice that truly hurts. Maybe this was our path…to take different roads. To learn from each other, we needed to grow separately.

The Girl iN the Red Dress

I was enjoying my life and becoming more self-aware of my changes. My personality and priorities had shifted. In February 2024 I started messaging with a girl. We had known about each other for years but had never met in person. Somehow, we started talking through Instagram. She was a Slovak girl living in Slovakia, and I was living in Ireland, building my life and career. We started chatting more, laughing together, enjoying each other's company even if it was only on screen. After a month we came up with the idea to meet in Katowice for a weekend.

I flew to Katowice, and she drove 250 km at night just to meet me. We agreed to meet at the hotel, because I didn't want her driving all the way to the airport. She didn't know the area, and I didn't want her to get lost or feel pressured.

I remembered what had happened already in Dublin. Maybe it was just coincidence, or maybe because I talk too much. At the airport, I heard two people speaking Polish near my gate. I asked them, "Sorry, are you flying to Katowice?" They said yes, and that's how our conversation started, beer in hand.

I told them I didn't know how to get to the city centre and asked if they had a taxi number or any advice, as the airport taxis are always overpriced. They told me, "Sorry, we don't really know the place well because we've just flown here." One of them said, "Wait, I'll call my friend. He's flying to Katowice too, and someone's picking him up. He might give you a lift." I thought that was so kind. I wasn't even in Katowice yet, and strangers were already helping me.

When I landed, a guy came up to me and said, "Are you Lukas?" I said yes. He explained he was the one picking me up, a friend of a friend. In no time I was in the city centre. His friend drove like he was racing against time. I thanked them for the lift, even asked how much he wanted, but he refused to take money.

Then I started walking down a long, wide street and I saw her. She wore a red dress, standing in the middle of a busy street. Red lipstick, red high heels, and this innocent look in her eyes, looking lost, searching for me. The girl who had driven through the night, hundreds of kilometres, just to see me.

That weekend we drank, laughed, went to restaurants, and enjoyed each other's presence. It felt good to be with someone who wanted me there. After that, we kept seeing each other often. It felt like the past was repeating, another long-distance, red dress, everything so quickly. Like something wanted to show me I would need this lesson. To learn what it takes to be with someone even far away. I believe if both people want it, anything is possible. I didn't want to fall in love, but it felt like the universe wanted to test me or maybe teach me something.

She had two kids. They liked me a lot, probably because I gave them my full attention. I played with them, listened to them, showed up like I believe every dad should. I spent every holiday with her and didn't even see my family.

From time to time, she went drinking with friends. It seemed casual, just a way to switch off her problems. We talked about life. She wanted to move out from her father's apartment. She dreamed of having her own place with me. I told her I would move to Slovakia by the end of the year. She was so happy, and I was happy too.

One night she told me she was going out with a friend I had met before. She promised to send photos and videos. She often did that, like she wanted to include me in her life even from a distance. She dressed up beautifully, makeup done. I complimented her and told her to enjoy the night. The next morning, I woke up to no messages. No notifications. Her phone was off. Worry started creeping in. Hours passed. Finally, around 11, my phone rang.

She said, "I was in the police station." My heart stopped. I asked if she was okay if her friend was okay. She said, "I'll tell you, but you can't say it to anybody because I could have a problem from it." My heart stopped again the moment she mentioned she was with her ex-boyfriend instead of the friend she told me about. She said it like it wasn't a big deal. Cold sweat flushed my body. Sadness filled my thoughts. Trust disappeared into silence. She said nothing happened between them, only drinking yet I couldn't believe it fully. I forgave her, but my mind kept returning to that night.

We started arguing. She hung up. Messages followed, blaming me for caring more about who she was with and what happened, instead of about her. She forgot that what happened was her choice or maybe it was easier to blame others. I told her she had to block him if she wanted me to trust her again. She did.

Still, something didn't feel right. She was drinking more. Maybe it was always there, and I hadn't seen it because I was blinded by my heart.

By August 2024, I told her I wouldn't move to Slovakia. Not because I didn't love her, but because I realised, I didn't have enough savings, I didn't have a job there, and I hadn't thought it through. I apologised and explained my vision of saving for a deposit so we could live securely in our own house. She kept repeating the same words "You promised me." The arguments grew and the love began to fade.

She said she couldn't trust me because I had lied to her and to her kids about moving. I think, we should always look in the mirror before we say something. I tried to explain myself; she didn't see me in that moment also she didn't hear my voice, only her vision of living. I remember many calls unanswered, nights away and now finally I know why. She was drunk, Still I loved her, but I didn't love the person she had become. Every time I tried to talk to her about it, she twisted my words. She called my truths "fantasy explanations." She said I was overanalysing but when things didn't make sense, I asked questions, just like a child and nothing made sense anymore.

I remember telling her once I was going to my aunt's birthday for two hours. Her response, "You're lying again. Who did you come to Slovakia for, me or your family?" That hurt deeply still I kept seeing the good in her. Her ex-husband was the most toxic man I had ever known, trying to destroy her at any cost. Maybe that's why I stayed, to show her some light but if she couldn't accept me visiting my aunt, that said a lot. I told her, "I'll never let anyone manipulate me again. I've been there before." Just like that she twisted the words against me, maybe because she wanted to hit me where it hurt the most.

Slowly we began to separate. It wasn't love anymore. It was constant fighting. Me trying to help her change. Her refusing to see any truth but her own.

It was November 2024. I was at the airport, flying back to Ireland, single. She called, crying. "My life is ruined. I made a huge mistake." I was in shock. What happened? She told me that she had been stopped by the police while drunk, with her child in the back seat. I calmed her down, told her that sometimes we make mistakes, but also said, this is your last chance to change. Tell the truth. Admit you have a drinking problem. She did, and then also to her family. She told others. She faced it for the first time in her life. I promised, I'd drive her to rehab if she signed up for it, that even though we weren't together, I'd still help.

I was proud of her. I know what it feels like when you think your life is over however maybe the truth is the only way forward, even if it's terrifying, even if it costs you people, even if it costs you the version of yourself you once protected. She once told me I was the only one who stood by her during her darkest moments. The only one who believed in her when she didn't believe in herself. I'm happy I could be that person. Not that I needed anything back, but because I saw the good in her, the part no one else saw, not even herself.

We cannot carry another's war with yesterday. Each soul must lay its own ghosts to rest. Choice is always there, but it can only rise from within. The truth is that the path is never easy, and it takes time. You may glimpse the light in another, but you cannot awaken them with your sight alone. They must come to see it for themselves.

So, I moved forward, not perfectly, but with clarity. Not with anger, but with growth. Not with blame, but with love. With the kind of love that starts with respect for myself.

I used to think love had to shake the earth beneath your feet to be real. That unless it felt like fire and chaos, it wasn't meant to last. I understand now that love is not something you find. Love is something you build. It grows in small moments, in patience, in trust, in showing up, in the quiet way someone says, "I'm here." It's not always loud. Not always magical still it's real, and maybe that's even more sacred.

For the first time, I'm not chasing what I lost. I'm learning to stay, to build, to be present in what I have. That, I think, is the beginning of a different kind of love, one that doesn't burn out.

I've come to understand that words are bridges. They can guide someone toward the quiet light of their dreams or close the door before they ever step through. If a single sentence can help one soul change its course, that is already success. Others have done the same for me, often without knowing, leaving small lanterns along my path but I've also learned that you cannot awaken someone who chooses to keep sleeping. Sometimes you're the only one reaching, because you see in them what they've forgotten, what they've buried deep. That doesn't mean they are bad, only that they are not yet in the place you stand. So, you must give your energy wisely, not only to protect your own flame but to protect your time, so it may be spent where it can truly grow.

WhEn Silence Spoke Back

*B*ack in Ireland, there was a quiet sadness in me. Not for what happened, but for her, for the way she chose to live her life.

On December 11th, I woke up in a sweat at 5 a.m. Not because I had to, but something inside me wouldn't let me sleep. The house was quiet, the kind of silence that presses against your ears, and outside the sky was still completely dark. It wasn't a nightmare that had woken me. It wasn't even a memory. It was simply a feeling, gentle but insistent. A voice without sound *"Send Jaya something. She needs it."*

At first, I almost laughed at myself. Why would I? We hadn't spoken in nearly two years. The last memory I had of our communication was silence and distance, the sort of ending that leaves more questions than answers. Yet the feeling was so strong, as if her energy had brushed against mine in the dark. I couldn't explain it logically, but it felt real, undeniable and for some reason, I trusted it.

So, I did something I hadn't done in a long time, nearly 2 years. I sent her a message yet not a short polite note. Not a casual *"Hope you're well."* What poured out of me that morning came from a deeper place, something raw and honest, unfiltered by fear or expectation. In that moment I had this feeling she needed to hear something good.

I reminded her of the strange, beautiful moments we shared, the kind that don't repeat, in the hope it would make her smile. I told her how much I valued the fact that she had opened her home and her safe space, to someone she barely knew, someone who could hardly even speak her language because she didn't have to, but she did.

I admitted something I had never said out loud, that she helped me discover myself. Not just in the ordinary way people help each other but in a way that reached way deeper in spiritually, emotionally. She was the mirror that showed me a side of myself I didn't know existed. She helped me to see, that anger was not an enemy but an ally and that's something I would always remember.

I didn't keep it heavy, that wasn't us. I added some of the ridiculous, funny moments that were so uniquely ours. I wrote about the time she went to Barcelona, and we spent days texting each other through Google Translate, creating the most broken conversations that somehow still made sense to us.

The truth was, beyond the memories, I only wanted her to remember one thing - a smile.

When I finally pressed send, I didn't expect anything in return. The peace came simply from writing it, from listening to that small whisper that told me she needed it. Later I remembered that she had blocked me. The message was never delivered, instead it vanished into digital silence I wasn't upset because the point was never about whether she read it or not, the point was sending it. Letting it exist in the space between.

A few days passed and still I couldn't help but wonder... why that morning? Why did the thought of her arrive so clearly, like an arrow through the fog? Even now, I can't explain it but I've come to believe that sometimes the soul whispers what the mind cannot. In rare moments, when we are still enough, we hear it.

That morning, my whisper was simple... *send it now.*

So, I did, though she never saw the words, I believe, somehow, somewhere, she felt them.

It was January 2025 when Ivan messaged me for my birthday. We spoke from time to time, nothing too deep, just casual conversations. I don't know why, but I had this random thought and asked him,

Do you have any plans for King's Day? Maybe we could meet... it's been a long time.

He said he wasn't in the Netherlands at the time, working remotely from another country, and wasn't sure if he'd be back home by then. I didn't push. I just told him there was a festival I'd always wanted to visit, Verknipt. He said he'd let me know closer to the time.

I agreed to wait, but in the meantime, I booked the flight anyway with a hotel. I promised myself, that even if I go alone, I'm going.

A few weeks later, near the end of February, I got a message, not the one I expected. I had to check twice to believe it. It was from Jaya. Out of nowhere. No warning. Just there.

Maybe that's why I had the urge to go back to the Netherlands; I couldn't tell but it felt like a sign.

She asked softly, maybe testing how I would react and whether we could still talk the way we once had. *"How are you? How's your colitis?"*

After all that silence, she couldn't have picked a better question. We started talking, and it felt like the separation had never existed. No fear. No tension. Just flow. Like we had picked up a paused conversation.

We laughed. We shared updates. She told me she had broken up with Roko. That he almost destroyed her. That she lost herself in that relationship and became someone she wasn't. I knew that feeling. I had lived it once, years ago, with someone who nearly shattered me.

I opened up a little too, told her where I'd been, how I'd changed. Then I mentioned something strange, how in December I had this sudden feeling that something was wrong. How I sent her a message, but it never delivered.

She was silent for a second. Then she said, *"That was the worst time of my life."*

She couldn't believe it. That was when the shop beside her caught fire, just a few meters from her house, and she had to evacuate with her kids. She told me she almost lost her soul then. That Roko was heavy, dark, and it nearly broke her completely inside.

That night we messaged each other for nearly two hours. It was strange because of what happened and how it happened. For the next few days, we kept talking. Not every day, but each time felt deep and honest. The kind of conversations where you don't need to pretend.

There was a feeling, but it was different now. I was changed and I wasn't sure about her yet somehow, the connection had never broken.

One day she asked me, "Do you think you'll ever feel the same for me again?"

I told her the truth of that moment those feelings never left.

I could sense her smile.

I mentioned the festival again and asked if she might want to come, to reunite after so long. She said she was too busy, and I understood. I didn't push.

We kept texting. She sent little pieces of her life, pictures, short videos from parties she went to. It felt like she wanted me to be part of her world again.

I started wondering again, is the twin flame real? I think it would explain everything but honestly, whatever it was, it was real.

In the meantime, Ivan and I agreed to go to the festival I had always wanted to see. The weeks passed quickly, and soon it was time to fly.

I was ready to see Ivan. Ready for the festival and stories that waiting for me in Netherland.

The Day the UniVersE Brought Us Back

*I*n April, I was back in the Netherlands. It felt like the universe was showing me the past in reverse. Same feeling with same path, but this time, I was different.

The moment I stepped into Schiphol Airport, something had shifted. I wasn't a stranger anymore. I didn't need signs to tell me where to go. I wasn't lost. It felt like I had come to a place I already knew, as if the ground remembered my steps. Excitement rose in me, not just for the festival, but for something deeper, a quiet joy carried by memory, whispering that I had been here before, that I had changed, but the path still remembered me.

I messaged Ivan to arrange where to meet, and in my usual way managed to go in the wrong direction before we finally found each other. He picked me up from the airport, and on the way to the hotel I asked if it would just be the two of us, half curious and half hopeful. He laughed and said, "Of course. Who else did you think I'd bring?"

We dropped our bags quickly at the hotel and were back out within twenty minutes. The festival wasn't far, and though the heat was intense we decided to walk.

Close to the place, the music was getting louder. It hit like a heartbeat, but this wasn't just music. It was an experience. The energy was unreal. Three stages, thousands of people, and somehow it all felt right, like I belonged inside the pulse of it. We danced, met a few people, tried the food. Hours passed until we stepped outside for air.

The chill-out area was filled with the smell of food stands, wooden tables crowded with strangers, people dressed in all kinds of ways, each one different yet beautiful. We sat down, lit a cigarette, and then something stirred inside me.

It wasn't a thought, not even a feeling. It was stronger than that. Like a pull or a whisper or even a force. "Look to the right now and so I did."

In the middle of the crowd, like a scene lifted out of memory and set down in front of me, Jaya. Everything slowed. Her face, her smile, her hair floating in the air, her energy, the tattoo on her arm I remembered as clearly as the day I first saw it. It was her.

I turned to Ivan and asked, barely able to speak, "Is that... Jaya?" He scanned the crowd, asked "Where?" and when I lifted my finger through the sea of people, he ran.

I stayed frozen, watching them talk for a moment, and then Ivan pointed back at me. Even from far away I could feel her eyes searching. When they found mine, the world changed.

It was like time had passed but hadn't touched anything essential, like she still knew me. She didn't walk. She ran.

The noise, the lights, the people, they all disappeared. The only real thing was her energy rushing toward me, as though the universe had been holding it in place for this exact moment. We embraced. Her arms wrapped around me, her warmth against my body, her cheek pressed to mine. It didn't feel like two years had passed. It felt like yesterday.

We kissed each other on both cheeks, a quiet collision of past and present, and then came her first words... "I missed you so much." The way she said it made the moment sacred.

"What are you doing here?" I asked.

She smiled softly. "I need a moment to believe this is real."

Her eyes met mine again, clear and alive, glowing just enough to undo me.

"Ivan knew I was coming. It was my plan but I didn't want to tell you. I wanted to surprise you." she did.

Our eyes stayed locked, and in that silence our energy spoke. It was recognition only souls understand.

We spent nearly the whole festival side by side. We danced, we laughed, she pulled me close, and every time our eyes met it felt as if we were looking into each other's soul. At one point we drifted away from Ivan and her friend Daniek without even realising it. Time stopped.

We talked about everything that had happened in the last two years, in her life and mine, how much we had both grown.

"It feels like you've changed, like you're calmer", she said. I told her I had started writing a book in January. She stared at me, wide-eyed, as if I had uncovered a secret she'd kept.

Why do you look so surprised? I asked.

"Because" she said, "I started writing a book in January too."

For a moment the world went still again. "This isn't coincidence. What are the chances?" we both said with laughter.

Her English was nearly perfect now. When I asked where she had learned, she smiled as though the answer was obvious, "You taught me."

We spent over an hour together without noticing the others searching for us. Later, when we went to order drinks, she translated every word for me, softly and naturally, as if it was the most normal thing in the world. It was like she was showing me she cared. She looked at me and said, "I can see you feel like home." In that moment maybe I did feel at home, it wasn't because of a place, it was because she was there. With her, in that moment, it felt like I did.

The day moved too quickly. One moment we were dancing and laughing, and the next the music slowed, the lights dimmed, and the crowd thinned. As we made our way out of the festival, she held my hand. The night was cold, so I gave her my sweater. She smiled and said, "Pretend to be my boyfriend so no one talks to me on the way out." We walked side by side, hand in hand, and in that moment, it didn't feel like pretending.

When it was time for our paths to separate, we hugged again. She held me tighter than before, as if her arms could delay the moment. Her eyes searched mine, and for a second neither of us wanted to let go. There were no big words left, just the weight of what wasn't said. Goodbye didn't feel like goodbye. It felt like see you soon.

Back at the hotel, I lay in bed replaying the day in my mind like a dream I didn't want to wake from. Staring at the ceiling, I whispered to the universe... "Is this how you planned it? What is the reason?" I wanted an answer, but strangely, deep inside, I felt it.

When the time is right, the universe will bring us back to where we stopped.

Maybe everything I imagined was only an illusion, a veil over the truth. Yet in that moment, it felt so real.

WheRe Something Else Began

When I returned to Ireland, something in me had shifted again. Like every time I crossed paths with Jaya, I evolved. I grew. It was as if I could see the world in a different way, more clearly. It wasn't just the memory of the festival or the way her eyes found mine. It was something deeper, a pull. Stronger than the one I had felt two years ago. More certain. More urgent.

It was like something inside me was whispering… *"This is it. Your time in Ireland is coming to a close. Be ready."* Ready for what? I kept questioning myself. Why did I feel like this? Why now, after seeing her again? I didn't have a logical answer. For the first time, I didn't need one. I began to trust my gut, my intuition, without knowing the outcome.

Two days later, I started crying. Out of nowhere. For two hours I sat in my room, no reason at all. I wasn't sad. I wasn't triggered. I just broke open. Jaya and I had been texting often since the festival, and I told her about it…the heaviness, the tears I couldn't explain. I asked her, *"Why am I crying like this?"* Neither of us could find an answer.

We spoke about spirituality, about the stages of awakening, and then she said, *"Maybe you're in a full awakening stage?"* I think she was right. I just didn't realise how deep it would go.

For five days straight, I cried. Randomly. Watching a comedy. Walking. Cooking a meal. It didn't matter where I was, something in me kept breaking free. Past pain became so clear, but it wasn't sadness. It was realization.

It felt as if every piece of my life was suddenly showing its meaning. Every choice. Every failure. Every heartbreak. Every delay. Every lost moment. Like a puzzle that had been waiting for all its pieces to be found. I was grateful, even for the pain, because I finally understood why it all had to happen the way it did.

Have you ever felt emotions so deeply that they flood you without warning? You begin to see your life, your patterns, your purpose, as if a blindfold has finally been removed and the moment truth hits, your body responds before your mind can catch up.

I felt it all. The release of illusions. The collapse of old beliefs. The quiet death of an old version of me. In its place came clarity, strength, and truth. A need to feel everything as it truly is. That's when *Something Else* truly began.

I don't know what label to give it - twin flames, soulmates, coincidence, or nothing at all. What I know is that some souls awaken you and change you without ever meaning to. They show you your light with your shadows. Sometimes it hurts and sometimes it doesn't but it is never to harm you-it is to reveal what still needs healing inside you. They push you to grow, to be honest and to rise that maybe, without even trying, you do the same for them. There may be silence, distance or separation but in those quiet spaces, the soul learns the most. It is a path of awakening and that is why it is worth it.

All I know is this… she came into my life for a reason. Not to stay, not to be mine, but to change me to bring me closer to who I was meant to be. The first time, I changed quietly and the second time, it was like light exposing truth through my whole body. She reminded me not by telling, but by being herself that I can love unconditionally, even without love being returned, and in that, I discovered my strength. That my heart is not too much and that one day will find someone to see it, to feel it.

Have you ever had a moment where you just stop? Not to regret, not to blame, but simply to see your life. To look at everything that happened, not with pain, but with peace. To feel grateful for the things you once cried over. To realise the very moments that nearly broke you were the same ones that shaped you. And somehow, you find yourself smiling through the same tears that once made you feel lost.

The One Who Said Yes

Maya and I had started messaging more often after our second meeting. There was no dramatic shift, just a quiet, natural rhythm. It felt like two people who had been hurt before, moving slowly now, with more care and less urgency. During one of our chats, she opened up about her struggles. She spoke about her perfectionism, her fears, her burnout, and her deep love for her two girls. I saw her clearly then, a woman doing everything she could, giving everything she had. When she doubted herself, I reminded her of her strength…and she smiled.

Around the same time, my mama was coming to visit me in Ireland. Three years had passed since her last visit, and just knowing she was on her way brought light into my home. She arrived on June 2nd, and what followed felt more like a dream than real life, not because it was too perfect but because of the strange, beautiful signs that started showing up like whispers from something bigger. We had the kind of week I'll never forget, full of stories, deep talks, late-night card games, and soft laughter that filled the quiet nights. It was beautiful, almost magical, to spend time with my mama like that. Something opened between us, something that hadn't before, a closeness beyond words.

One evening, I asked her about her childhood, about our grandparents. As she spoke, I could see it in her eyes, the light, the joy, the softness. It was as if my questions carried her back to a time when she was still a child, to that little world she once called home.

A few nights later, as the week was ending, another part of my story quietly began to turn. I casually mentioned to Jaya that I'd be visiting her city in August and said it would be nice to see her again. She told me she'd be away with her kids, but then realised her holiday was actually the week before. Then she asked something unexpected, "Do you have any other summer holidays planned?"

I did. Back in December 2024, Shane, one of my best friends, had invited me on a summer trip with his family planned for 2025. The original idea was to go to Greece, but when we voted, seven out of eleven chose Italy. I wasn't one of them. Shane's sister Louise, who took full responsibility for organizing everything, decided on Agrigento as our destination. The dates were set for June 22 to 26. Then Jaya told me she had booked a solo trip to Malta from the 20th to the 23rd of June.

We stared at the dates. Two trips. Same weekend. Countries just across the sea from each other. I checked the map and just stared. She asked, *"You could come earlier?"* I joked, *"If you find me a bed, I'll check the flight."* The next day she messaged me, *"U welcome,"* and sent me a link to book a room in her hotel.

I didn't have the extra money, and I didn't expect she would say yes and invite me either. I told my mama everything, not because I had to, but because she was the one person I could tell everything to without feeling crazy or foolish. I told her about the signs, the strange timings, the gut feeling I couldn't explain. We looked at each other. Tears came. Not from sadness, but from knowing. We both started to cry but for different reasons. She saw how much it meant to me because she believed me. I asked her why she was crying, and she simply said, *"Because I want you to be happy, and to find out what this is all about. You're not going there for her; you're going there for yourself."*

It was the purest form of love and wisdom, from someone who had stood by my side since the beginning. Someone who had seen my first steps, my first words, my first troubles, my first everything. Even after so many years, she still supported me and always wanted me to be happy. She helped me pay…and I booked it.

Later, Jaya sent me a party invite for a beach event in Malta on June 21st. Strict white dress code. I only had a white shirt. The next day, my mama said, *"Let's check in town. Maybe we'll find something."* We walked into a shop. There was one pair of white pants. Perfect fit. She laughed and said, *"Lukas... this was meant to happen."* That same day, I learned something else. June 21st is the summer solstice, the longest day of the year, when the sun is closest to Earth.

My thoughts… two people in white, dancing on a beach in Malta. Not planned, not forced. Just aligned. If we had booked different places, it wouldn't have happened. If my mama hadn't visited, I wouldn't have shared the signs. If she hadn't believed, I wouldn't have gone.

This time, I kept it quiet. No big announcements, no mentioned anything to my best friends. No telling the world, some moments don't need an audience. They need silence and trust.

So many times, I thought I was lost and so many moments I doubted myself, but something always stayed. A thread. A pull. A quiet knowing.

When my mama came, something shifted. A week of magic signs, beliefs and tears that weren't from sadness, only from knowing that somehow, without realizing it, she became a witness and my guide in one. The one who said yes when I almost said no.

So, there I went, flying to Malta. Not to chase her, but to step into the moment itself. To search for the missing piece of the puzzle, the one that might finally show me who I am. To meet myself, whole and unafraid.

The Altar I Never Knew I Built

The day I brought my mama back to the airport, something inside me cracked open.

We had spent a week together, full of laughter, deep conversations, soft support, quiet understanding, and quiet happiness not said but felt. A rare week. A needed one.

We didn't even get to say a proper goodbye at the airport. No kiss on the cheek. No whispered *see you later*. It wasn't her fault. I remember her turning back and looking at me, like she was lost and I was the one who couldn't follow her after she passed the ticket check. I wanted to walk her through the check-in so badly, just to hold her hand one more time. My tears started to show, so I ran back to the car before she could get upset too.

Five minutes into the drive home, I had to stop the car. The tears came like a storm. Not gentle. Not slow. Raw. Replaying the whole week with my mama, hearing her voice, her laugh, remembering the small moments that now felt too big to hold.

I called Itta, the person I trust deeply. She knows every corner of me. She stayed with me on the phone for the entire two-hour drive.

Quiet sometimes, but present. Like a soul anchor. I felt grateful that even when I collapse, love catches me.

When I got home, I called her and said "Okay, I'm home" with a laugh in my voice. However, when I hung up and stepped out of the car, memories came rushing. I couldn't walk into the house. I couldn't go into my room. The silence was too loud. So, I walked. Not because I had a destination, but because standing still would have broken me more.

Later that day, once mama arrived back home, we spoke again, and I found peace. Not just because I heard her voice, which always straightens my path, but because of what she said. I don't remember the exact words, but I remember this… everything had a purpose. Maybe her visit wasn't just comfort, maybe it was something bigger. A trigger or a turning point I didn't fully see yet but was waiting for me to find out.

In the corner of my room were two broken bracelets, shattered months ago. All that remained were the loose stones. One was from my mama, one from my sister, both given to me the Christmas two years ago. One for love. One for protection.

They had sat untouched in a stone charging bowl for nearly a year. Until that day.

I don't know why, I just felt a sudden pull. I decided to rebuild them, not exactly as they were.

I mixed the stones. Let intuition guide my hands. I made two new bracelets, each with 22 stones, accidentally. I only counted them after I finished. I sealed them with a lighter, not knowing why, and placed them back into the bowl.

An hour later, Jaya messaged me. Out of nowhere.

She said she felt strange. Maybe it was the full moon coming. I hadn't even known one was near.

So I looked it up.

Strawberry Moon.

Not just any moon, but one of the lowest on the horizon in two decades.

A moon that would rise just 11 days before Malta, on June 21st, the longest day of the year, when the sun reaches its highest point.

When I realised it, I was speechless. I never told her about the bracelets. Maybe it was sacred. Spiritually, I'd read that rebuilding bracelets and placing them under moonlight can mean preparing your soul for something big. Letting go of the past but keeping what's still alive in you. It's alignment. It's trust. Maybe even whispering from the universe…*You will be whole soon.*

Later that night, I showered in silence. A candle lit near the sink, soft music in the background. Time blurred.

When I stepped out, the motion light didn't turn on. Instead, I saw tiny lights scattered across my chest, like stars briefly printed on my skin. It wasn't the candle's reflection. This was different.

I took a photo. The image still shows them.

The next day, I couldn't stop thinking about it. I showed Jaya. I wasn't even thinking about her reaction, how strange it might sound, yet she didn't laugh. She didn't brush it off. She listened. She understood. She made me feel seen. Like I wasn't crazy. Like I was trusted.

She told me she was planning a ritual too, a cleansing, to let go of what no longer served her.

I told her about the Strawberry Moon, how rare it was. We both just paused. Could this all be coincidence, I wondered?

Malta didn't feel like a vacation. It felt written, but why? For who? What purpose? I kept asking myself deep down.

The next day, it felt like something was blooming between us, quietly. Not on the surface, but beneath it. As if our souls were writing their own dialogue, beyond what our minds could understand.

She messaged, "Nobody gonna fuck up our holidays!"

It made me smile, one of those real smiles that warm your chest.

Later that night, I don't know why, I asked her, "Did you ever see the cover of my book?"

She hadn't, I asked her to tell me not what she thought of it, only what she felt. The moment I sent her the cover, she said one word,

"Woow". No more words, just a little silence, a pause of feeling, and for me, that was enough.

We joked afterwards, sent playful messages, a countdown reminder... only six days to go.

I thought this isn't just a trip. It's a turning point written not by hand, but by something else.

It was Friday, my first day back at work after three weeks of recovery.

I still felt fragile from the colitis flare, in both body and mind and I couldn't focus. Maybe it was the medication or maybe it was everything else, the emotions, the realisations, the weight of invisible truth rising all at once.

Then Jaya messaged me. She said something had just happened, right near our hotel in Malta.

A building had collapsed.

No one was hurt, thank God...still, it shook me.

I thought... maybe that's why I'm going there. To the place where something fell, so I can rise. To a place of old stories, where I will write a new one.

The next morning, I walked to the corner of my room, to the little windowsill where I'd been placing random things over the years...at least, that's what I used to think.

There was a small golden pyramid I bought last year. I had no idea why. Now, something made me look again. I noticed the symbol on it... light, spirit, body. I googled it. *Merkaba*. Something inside me shifted. Next to it was a tiny angel holding a heart I found five years ago. The bracelets I had just rebuilt. A star that fell from my wall map, but I placed it there instead of back on the wall, like it knew. A love poem. I can't even remember where it came from.

I realised...my windowsill wasn't just a shelf. This wasn't decoration. It was a living altar my soul had built without me noticing, slowly, piece by piece, over years. Every object a symbol of hope, memory, timing, and love.

I broke down in tears. Not out of sadness, but because of how much I finally saw. The truth hit hard. Nothing had been random. The universe had been speaking all along. I just hadn't known how to listen.

That same evening, I don't know why, but I messaged Jaya and asked if she wanted to read a chapter from my book, the one I wrote after we met again, after years of silence.

She replied instantly, *"Yesss!!"*

As I sent the chapter, my heart beat like a drum. I started to worry, but now when I look back, I know I shouldn't have. I wasn't just sharing my writing, I was handing her a mirror into my soul.

I waited. Then her message came, *"I'm kind of scared again."*

Followed by another message, *"Do you think we belong together as partners?"*

She said the story was well written, but her question hung in the air. I felt the energy shift, subtle but real.

I knew this was my moment. To stay small as I always did before, or... speak truth.

So, I answered, not with logic or strategy, but letting my heart take over the words. I do feel a different connection between us. Something I can't explain. Too many coincidences I can't ignore. I'm not trying to control it, I'm just letting it unfold, because it feels meant to be, but I do understand if it sounds too much.

Then came silence. Hours passed. It felt heavy, like the past was trying to touch me again, whispering... "don't be who you are. It's a shame to be this way. To be open is too much".

Finally, she wrote, *"I feel sick this evening. Just threw up."*

...then, nothing!

I thought, that's it. I scared her away. She didn't understand I tried to honour our connection. She saw it differently, as if old wounds in me still showed, little pieces I thought I had healed. My mind spun with regret, yet my heart felt lighter because I didn't betray myself. I was honest.

Then the next message came, and it didn't hurt. It healed.

She said, "I want to be honest with you. I do feel a nice connection, a sense of trust and openness, and I truly appreciate that, but I don't feel anything romantic. I need to be clear, I don't want to create confusion or lead you on. I really value the way we talk and your openness. You're a beautiful person, just not someone I see as a partner."

She then sent a photo of a heart rate monitor, flat, quiet, with a smile, "I'm dying," she said, adding the kind of smile you didn't need to see to know it was there.

Her humour, still alive. Still shared.

Just like that, nothing lost. Just something transformed.

Truth became the bridge between us, not the barrier.

Something was coming. So here I was, holding the stones from bracelets that had broken long ago. Rebuilding what once was. Trusting something I couldn't see.

This wasn't just about planning a trip. This was about remembering. I wasn't sure if the signs were good or bad, but I knew they meant something. Maybe something to learn. Maybe something to understand. About her. About me.

Now, I'm packing, and this doesn't feel like a holiday.

It feels like a return to a version of myself that never gave up. To a feeling that never left. To a promise that stayed silent, but alive.

Sometimes we think we're building something in front of us, but instead, it may be something we are being built from. Simple things we pass each day, their meaning fading into the ordinary, until we forget they were ever sacred. They may not seem like much, because they live inside the everyday, and so their meaning slips away. Yet they are the greatest treasures hidden in plain sight.

A Place of Truth

When I lit the candle that night before the flight, I didn't wish for anything. I just thanked whatever force carried me here to find out. Two candles had become a part of my life by now, not just one I carried for the last 14 years for my nanny every night, but one also for me. For the boy who once walked alone, and for the man who kept walking, even when it hurt.

I was sitting at Dublin Airport. Gate 111. The same gate I flew from two years ago to the Netherlands. Same silence, but everything felt different now, not because of where I was going, but because of who I had become.

There was something quiet in me. Not numb. Not excited. Just… still. Like my heart wasn't rushing anymore. Like it already knew something was about to happen.

We didn't plan it this way, yet I think deep down, we both felt it. This was a question we never asked out loud. A question both of us needed to know the answer to… *"what is this connection… really?"*

I looked around that gate and felt something strange. Like time had bent just enough to give me this moment. Like everything I had doubted, feared, hoped for was leading me right here, even though I didn't know the reason yet, I knew I'd find out soon.

Malta

The flight felt endless not because of the hours, but because of what was waiting on the other side or maybe it all comes from an excitement that was still holding me

When I landed, the sun hit me, warm, golden, but soft. It didn't shout. It whispered... *"You made it. You're ready now to see."*

I stood in arrivals, looking for her. Then my phone buzzed.

"Where are you?"

"I'm waiting at arrivals. Where are you?"

"I'm already outside."

I blinked. How did I miss her? I rushed out, tried to find her and then I saw her. For a moment, I couldn't believe it. We met again.

After all the silence. All the time. We weren't strangers. Maybe not quite the people we once were. Maybe the covers look the same but inside we were different and still, I think we met in the exact place our souls always meant to.

We booked a taxi from the airport and headed to the hotel. In the back seat, something softened. We were laughing, trying to believe this was real, that we were here. It felt easy for a moment. Familiar. Like we had pressed pause on the world and picked up right where we left off, only somewhere new.

When we arrived, we checked in and dropped our bags. I was starving. I looked at her and said, "Let's go get something to eat. We've got a long night ahead."

We had two things booked, a boat trip at 17:30, and later, a moon pool party at one of the tallest buildings in Malta. We were meant to float between sea and stars.

We found a little place nearby for lunch. Ordered a few drinks, shared some food. I offered to pay, I said it was a welcome present. Time moved fast. After lunch, we went back to the hotel to get ready. Outfits changed. Perfume. That quiet excitement of going out with someone you've been waiting to see.

We walked toward the boat dock, arriving around 17:15. There was a big boat leaving, filled with people. I laughed. "Imagine if that's our boat."

Then it hit me. It was. It left without us.

I checked the ticket again. It said 17:30, but it didn't matter, it was gone.

We stood there for a second, then laughed, not the kind that fixes anything, just the kind that says, well… what can you do? At least we still had the party to look forward to.

SomethinG Shifted

After missing the boat, we walked to a nearby bar that looked out over the sea. The heat was too much, so we ordered cocktails, anything cold.

Jaya kept asking me to take pictures of her. At first, I laughed, warning her I wasn't much of a photographer. I joked that with me behind the camera she might end up with photos where half her head was cut off or where the focus landed more on the floor than on her. I said people would probably wonder if I'd been drinking before I even picked up the phone. She rolled her eyes, laughed, and still insisted, so I kept clicking away like some reluctant tourist guide tricked into a side job, but after a few shots, it started to feel like I was there more for the photos than for the holiday together.

As we kept talking, something felt different after all the rush of everything, now in the quiet with only the sound of the waves around us, I realised it that the conversation didn't flow like before. It was as if a space had opened between us, one I didn't know how to cross.

Maybe it was the chapter I had sent her before this trip, the one where I wrote about how I felt after we met at the festival, after two years of silence. Maybe she still carried it in her mind, not knowing what to say, pretending everything was the same as before, I couldn't tell.

I felt the shift. It was like standing beside someone who had once been close but now felt far away. Maybe it was because I had changed in the quiet time, and our messages had only been a shadow of what once was yet in the present, where nothing hides behind a screen, it was undeniable. Two souls that had once met in the same rhythm now moving to different ones, no longer finding each other in the same place. I stayed quiet, holding the moment gently, breathing it in, trying to make the most of what was left, even as I knew something had already slipped away.

The Party That Wasn't

Once we arrived back at the hotel, we changed clothes and got ready for the moon party. After I booked a taxi, we were on our way. In the car, while we imagined what the party would be like, I didn't feel like myself. It was as if I was pretending to be someone who matched the vibe aversion of me from before and it felt like a conflict was rising inside me. The new me against the old one. I thought I had buried that version long ago, and yet somehow it was trying to surface again.

We arrived too early, so we walked around the city centre to see what was there. We stopped for coffee and cake. I paid again, without her even offering. It wasn't about the money, but something in the silence of it stayed with me.

We wandered into a nearby bar where music was already playing. It wasn't packed, but it had a vibe. We grabbed drinks and took a table. That's when she started acting strange. Every time I leaned in to dance with her, she pulled away.

"Don't come near me," she said, waving her finger at me.

It stung. Not because I expected anything from her, but because I didn't understand. We were two friends at the same table, yet it felt like we were sitting on opposite sides of a wall. I didn't know how to act.

I started questioning myself. Can I say this? Can I ask that? I began to feel a little afraid to be myself, worried she might say something again to push me away. She kept looking around, and I noticed she was trying to catch the attention of the men around us. This was the first time I saw something in her I hadn't seen before, the way she acted, presenting herself. Not enjoying the present, not sharing the moment with me, but scanning the room as if deciding who else she might talk to.

I didn't mind, honestly. It confused me because we came here together. I thought this would be our time to reconnect, to talk, to laugh. Instead, it felt quiet. Distant.

Later, we walked over to the moon pool party we had planned. There were barely any real conversations between us. No catching up. No deep moments. Just smiles for the camera and drinks I paid for.

I felt it building in my chest that quiet kind of sadness that doesn't scream, it just sinks. The realization that maybe I wasn't even the friend I thought I would be. Or maybe she wasn't the same person I had once known, but then why invite me to Malta at all?

The party filled up quickly, but the crowd was so young, mostly early twenties. She leaned in and said, "Let's go, it's full of kids."

I didn't mind the age because I believe fun doesn't need permission, yet it felt like she was searching for something we weren't going to find there.

We left, slipping back into the night, returning to the first bar where it had all begun only this time, it didn't feel like the beginning anymore. Something between us had shifted, and deep down I knew it wouldn't shift back.

The TurnIng Point

The place was full now, the air thick with noise. Loud music. Louder energy. Lights flashed across the room as bodies moved in every direction, voices shouting to be heard above the beat. We found a spot near a group of guys. One of them kept looking at her, and she kept looking back.

After a few drinks, I started dancing again. A girl came over and began moving with me. For a moment, it felt light, easy, like maybe I could forget everything and just let go, but before anything could happen, Jaya joined us, sliding into the space between us, and the girl slipped away.

I was left confused by her signals. She kept going to the toilet, always staying there for a while, vanishing for long stretches. After a couple of her disappearances, we went outside for a smoke, but even there something felt off. She kept her distance and even raised her hand to signal me not to come closer again. We were sitting behind two different tables, and in that moment, it felt like we were sitting in two different worlds. Me, confused, her… I don't know.

Instead of enjoying the holiday, I started doubting myself. Maybe I was standing too close. Maybe even as a friend, I was too much. When she finally came back from the toilet, she said, "There's this guy who always talks to me when I go to the toilet."

"That's perfect. Maybe you have a catch," I replied, with smile happily for her but in my mind, I was somewhere else and felt alone

A few minutes later she went again, this time, she didn't come back. I sat alone for thirty minutes with a drink while the group of guys laughed, one of them even pointing at me.

I messaged her, *"Where are you? Are you okay?"*. There was no reply. So, I messaged again, *"I'm heading back to the moon party. Gonna check there"*.

I met a few people at the party, I danced to release the tension inside me. When I dance, I'm not trying to impress anyone. I just let go. The music moves through me like light through water. I disappear into truth. People came over, gave me hugs, told me I was a great dancer. One group even moved an entire table to make space for me, and of course, I didn't reject it. For a while, I felt free. For a while, I remembered myself.

After around an hour, I checked my phone. Still nothing. I started to worry. I think anyone who cares would. I messaged her again, *"Are you still in the bar we were at together? I'm coming back"*.

As I stood outside the bar, a message finally appeared, *"Have a good night"*.

That was it. No explanation. No question. Just silence dressed as goodbye. Somehow, I knew it wasn't only for that night.

I walked back inside, still hoping for something. The same group of guys saw me and laughed again. Then, I saw her talking to one of them beside the bar. Smiling. Happy.

I walked up, trying to stay calm. She looked at me and said, "Where have you been? This is Tomas." I shook his hand and said hello with smile. He seems to be a good guy but inside, something was breaking and her words landed right on time like a truth I didn't see.

I looked at her and said, "You know what, Jaya…" That's when the new version of me stepped in and stopped me from saying more. I just walked away.

Was I angry? Yes, a little. Not from jealousy, but from being forgotten. To be ignored. To be left alone. I wanted to ask why, but

I didn't want to sound like too much. Maybe because she always told me I was.

So, I went and grabbed something to eat. Something simple. Something to help me forget that moment and remind myself to enjoy where I was. When the hunger was gone, so was the sadness. What replaced it was truth.

The Light I Carry

I messaged her, *"I feel tired. Enjoy your night. I'm heading back to the hotel."*

With a smile emoji, like nothing happened. So, she could enjoy her night.

The taxi ride was silent, yet not empty. Full of everything I wasn't able to say.

I didn't cry, I didn't scream. I just sat with it,

and slowly, the ache began to shift into something else. Something like understanding.

I stopped at the little shop near the hotel and bought water and chocolate. Earlier in the day, we had joked that we'd need them for the hangover, and I left them outside her door. Not because I had to but because that was who I was.

I took a photo and sent it with a message, *"I think this one will help when you get back."*

Just a small gesture. Just me. Always soft, even when things feel heavy.

Later, she messaged me, *"I feel like you were angry."*

I told her the truth, *"Yes, I was. You left me alone. I'm happy you found company for yourself, but do you remember the story you once told me? When your friend left you alone at a party for someone else, and how bad it made you feel? You did the same thing to me."*

She replied that I couldn't compare the two. That her party had been much bigger.

I told her that *it wasn't about the size of the party. It was about the principle. I would never leave a friend alone, especially not if I invited them and if I ever had to step away, I'd let them know where I was, so they wouldn't feel abandoned or worry that something had happened."*

I didn't write it to hurt her. I wrote it because it was true…because I needed to say it.

When I got back to my room, I lay on the bed, replaying the whole night. Thinking of the moments I should have left, and the moment everything shifted.

That's when I started to see the truth. It didn't break me. It reminded me of who I am, and who I've become.

Piano music played softly in the background. Instead of sadness, peace began to rise. Instead of fear, something lighter flowed in.

My heart wasn't hurt anymore, because I noticed the little things around me, how strangers made me smile, how a simple gesture could lift the mood.

I was in Malta, a place I hadn't planned, yet I was alive in it.

The night hadn't gone how I hoped, but maybe it had always been written this way, that meant something.

Life isn't measured by perfect nights. It's measured by how you carry yourself through the imperfect ones.

I remembered the candle, the gate, the quiet stillness before the flight.

The light had never left me. It was mine to carry.

The Last Dance Was for Me

It was the day of the White Party, the 21st of June. I didn't know if we would go together or if I'd end up on my own, making my own plans.

Around lunchtime her first message arrived, sharp at first, almost blame, but I chose to keep the lightness there, not letting the day turn into a bad memory. Slowly, she softened, a smile returning between the words. Then she said, *"Okay, we'll take our little journey first and then go to the party."*

I didn't refuse. That had been the plan all along.

We booked a taxi for 7:30 evening. I had told her I wanted an hour to myself at sunset, that I didn't want to miss it. She gave me instructions, when to begin, how to time it, reminding me we wouldn't see each other until then.

At 7:15, there was a knock. I opened the door, and she was standing there. Her expression wasn't distant, it carried something else, a softness, almost a wanting. The way her eyes lingered on me felt different, as if she were suddenly drawn to a side of me she hadn't noticed before. For a moment, I could feel it. She liked what she saw, maybe even wished to be closer.

In my eyes, for the first time, she seemed human. Not the girl who once felt like fire, not the energy I had been drawn to so fiercely, not the magnetic spark I remembered. Just human.

She had once told me that certain journeys strip away illusions, that they let you see a person for who they truly are inside. Maybe, just maybe, that's what I was seeing now.

When we arrived, we drifted apart. She stayed waiting at the party gate. I walked to the beach, chasing the sunset.

On the shore, where waves touched the sand and the sky turned to gold, not to dazzle but to soften me. The longest day of the year. As if the universe wanted to give me just a little more light before letting me go. I stood with the sun melting at the edge of Malta, two bracelets on my wrist, no longer asking who they were for but simply knowing. One was mine. The other, a memory of who I was.

In that moment, as the sea breathed slowly and the light poured everything it had into its final hour, I pressed play. *Misty Mountains* by Leyna Robinson's voice floated into the fading sky. I knew why it was that song. Because something in me had travelled far. Through shadows. Through silence. Through love not fully returned. Finally, I was coming home.

Not to her, but to myself.

I was at peace. Not because I wasn't feeling, but because I had already felt everything. I just stood there. Still, alive, free in that final sunset, on the longest day the light ever stayed with me, I wasn't alone, I was with me.

The waves slowed, showing me the reflection of the sun falling, the sky and the sea speaking softly of how much this moment would change, not just around me, but within me.

One hour later, when I returned to the party in peace, I found her standing alone by a table. I walked over and asked if she wanted something to drink. She gave me a small smile and said, "I'm going to the toilet, I'll be back soon."

When she left, I turned toward the bar. I didn't wait for her anymore. Instead, I ordered a drink and let the music surround me. I sent her one simple message, *"When you're back, let me know."*

She returned a little while later and we exchanged only a few words, nothing more than a short chat yet the music was calling me to freedom, so I went to dance.

That was the moment last time I saw her.

Looking back, there were times I thought I had lost everything, Yet, still, I found myself.

There were moments I waited for someone to save me, but the truth is, no one came.

I became the one I was waiting for.

I used to think I was too much.

Too sensitive.

Too intense.

Too lost.

Now I understand.
I was never too much.
I was just tuned into things others hadn't noticed yet.
I was never broken.
I was just being reshaped.
Maybe you are too.
Maybe, just maybe, we're not here to win or prove or fix anything.
Maybe we're here to feel.
To grow.
To remember.
Then to leave traces of that remembering behind.

So, if you're wondering where your path is going, I'll tell you what I tell myself… keep going. Keep softening, even when it hurts. The universe always answers, but only when you're brave enough to ask with your heart wide open.

When it all falls apart again, because sometimes it will, don't forget… that's when the light gets in.

That night, I sat alone by the water. The truth landed again, soft but undeniable. From joy, from surrender, from knowing that this story was never about endings.

It was about coming back to yourself, through another. Maybe that's what Jaya really was. Someone I was meant to find, to find me.

Malta didn't just help me let go. It helped me see, not through love, or memory, or hope, but through truth.

For a long time, I thought we were the same kind of different like two old souls, two seekers, but we weren't. We were something else entirely.

I loved her spark, laughter, and her light but I mistook that spark for depth. I think she mistook my depth for danger. She reached out and pulled away in the same breath. I was steady. I stayed. Even in silence.

We weren't speaking the same language. I spoke through reflection. She spoke through reaction. This isn't blame. It's release.

We were never meant to become something. We were meant to wake something up in each other. I think, or I hope, we did. She lit the fire that burned away my illusions. I showed her a depth she wasn't ready to hold.

That was our purpose. That was our end.

I don't carry it as a wound anymore, but as a turning point. A sacred mismatch that brought me back to myself.

I don't cry when I write now. Not because the feeling is gone, but because it finally has a place to rest.

In the beginning, every word felt like pulling pieces of myself from the past, raw, unfinished, and full of ache. The tears came without warning, not because I wanted them, but because I couldn't stop them. The truth was too big to hold in, and it hit harder than I ever expected. Now, I look back at the words, and I see him. The man I was, the one who didn't yet understand and who had to feel it all to finally see. I don't cry for him anymore. Because he made it through, and maybe this silence in my chest isn't emptiness. Maybe it's peace.

Destiny in Motion

Jaya didn't come to say goodbye. Not to the little restaurant where we first shared a coffee. Not to the reception where we once walked in together.

I waited, suitcase by my side, as the taxi pulled in to take me to the port. The plate read 111, a sign that seems to follow me. Once, it was Gate 111 a plane taking me to her. This time, it was a taxi taking me away, a quiet confirmation that my part in this chapter was complete.

I knew it in my bones… this was the last time we would speak. A part of me ached, yes, but another part was calm. I didn't need to hold on. She had been part of my becoming, turning me from a man of illusion into a man of presence. Not hardened, but whole.

A man who finally found himself without closing his heart. Maybe I understand now. Maybe that was always her way, to leave without closing doors, to protect herself. Whatever it was, it was her choice. To live the life she knew. Maybe with fear. Maybe just behind walls.

Her last message came just before I sat in the taxi, *"Can you send me all the photos you have of us?"* I sent them. She thanked me…then… silence, the kind that says more than words ever could.

Just as I stepped onto the ship, another message arrived. The same words she had used nearly two years ago, *"I will block you."* Once, it would have broken me. I would have stared at the screen, wondering what she meant. This time, it didn't even land. I didn't reply. I just locked the screen. Not out of anger, but because I had already walked through that door. The truth had been waiting for me all along, and now I could finally see it.

The ship began to move, slowly pulling away from Malta. I stepped out onto the deck to see it one last time, to breathe it in. That ancient island in the middle of the Mediterranean, warm, still, holding so much of my story. Malta carried her shadow, but it also carried my becoming.

I looked at the soft gold of the buildings, at the quiet stillness of the evening, and at the version of me standing there now. Not bitter. Not lost. Changed. Grateful for all that had happened, for all that had broken me open, just so I could meet myself more deeply.

As the island faded into the horizon, I whispered... thank you. For her. For all of it.

Then I turned toward the sea, unclear but endless, and something in me exhaled. For the first time in a long while, I felt free. Not thinking about what might come next. Just here, calm, with a smile.

Something inside whispered… It's time. Time to trust. Time to believe.

I didn't know what Sicily would bring. I didn't know who I'd meet, or what it would stir inside me. A new place. A new chapter. Maybe a new version of me, stepping into the unknown not with fear, but with an open heart.

As a song once said, *"There is destiny in motion."* All I had to do was let it unfold.

I knew, deep inside that I was not lost anymore. I was ready.

Stars in the Sea

Back then, I didn't see it coming. How Sicily would become a place where each day held its own meaning, and each one quietly stayed with me.

When I arrived, my friends Shane and his sister Louise were still two hours away, since the cruise had docked earlier than expected. I had mixed up the time. Looking out at the land, a place I didn't know yet but one that would end up giving me so much, I found a small restaurant by the beach.

The staff were kind and polite. I ordered a drink and asked if I could leave my bag while I went for a walk. The waiter didn't hesitate. I took off my shoes and walked toward the sea.

It felt different from anywhere I had been before. Peaceful. Maybe because of what had just happened in Malta. Maybe because, for the first time, I was at peace with myself.

Time passed quickly. When my phone rang, joy rose quietly inside me. It was Shane.

"Where are you, bro?" he asked.

I laughed. "I'll be the eejit strutting down the middle of the road with sunglasses on and a backpack, looking like I own Sicily."

Seeing them filled me with happiness, especially knowing how tired he must have been after driving two hours just to collect me. The drive to Agrigento felt like a never-ending story, but we finally made it. Across from the hotel, the lads were waiting in a restaurant. By midnight the kitchen was closed, but the beers were cold, gold in the heat of the night.

When I saw them all, I couldn't believe it. A big Irish family, my second family, gathered on holidays. They welcomed me with warm hugs and bright smiles. That moment stays forever in my heart.

The next morning, I woke early. Not because I wanted to, but because the heat had already crept in, and maybe also because of excitement. After breakfast I went straight to the pool. It should have been filled with splashes and laughter, but it was quiet.

The hotel felt untouched, as if the world had forgotten to send guests. As if the universe whispered, *"Let him have this. He's earned the stillness."* No lines, no rush for sunbeds. Just blue water, calm as glass, and a sky so clear it looked like a new beginning. I pressed my shoe into warm stones and let the silence rest on me. Not empty. Present.

Maybe peace doesn't always come from others. Maybe sometimes you need the absence to hear your own heart whisper… *"You're doing okay."*

That day we visited an ancient site in the mountains of Agrigento. It was beautiful, but we had chosen the hottest part of the day for a three-hour tour. By the time the 32-degree heat wrapped around us, it was too late to turn back. I was reapplying sun cream every thirty minutes like holy water and still wasn't sure it worked. We roasted, sweated, and laughed our way through like heat-struck pilgrims. By the end, I wasn't looking for souvenirs, just a cold beer and the air-conditioned car. Red faces, tired feet, and memories worth keeping. Life isn't perfect, but it's the little moments that make you smile.

That evening we asked our taxi driver to take us to the best restaurant in town. We believed him like tourists believe everything said with an accent, but when we arrived, the place was closing. No food, just cocktails. So, we treated the cocktail list like the menu and drank as if it were a tasting mission. Hunger forgotten. Priorities realigned.

On the way back I started singing an Italian song I had been humming all week. None of us knew the words, not even close, but that didn't stop us. We sang like a choir of tone-deaf gladiators. The performance was unforgettable. I'm sure the driver still tells the story.

That's when I had the idea. "Let's go for a night swim in the sea when we get back to the hotel."

That night something magical happened. A few of us went. The water was warm, and the deeper I went, the more I saw it. Light sparking between my fingers. At first, I thought it was reflection, but it wasn't. The sea itself was alive with stars.

"Hey, look!" I shouted. "There's light in the water when you move!"

It felt like swimming in the universe, drifting among stars in silence, with bursts of light beneath the surface. As if the universe was preparing me for what was coming or reminding me of something I hadn't yet understood.

I turned onto my back, let the water carry me, ears filled until all I could hear was silence, and stared at the sky. In that moment, silence became a melody, and the soul could see clearly through the eyes.

I whispered, "Thank you, for this little moment."

It felt as if the universe itself was saying... *You are exactly where you are meant to be, on the path you were always meant to walk.*

The Quiet Shine

The next morning, an Italian group came by the pool, maybe eight or ten of them. They were all happy, beautiful, enjoying their moment together. One of the girls, I don't know why, stood out for me. There was something about her. She was quietly different, not because of how she looked, but in the way her presence gently shone.

It wasn't attraction even though she was beautiful. It was something else I couldn't quite describe. There was a quiet strength in her. A softness that wasn't weak, but steady. A flame that didn't look for attention, and she didn't try to show it either. It was simply there.

I wasn't paying much attention. I was with my group, enjoying the morning, and from time to time, I looked at her. Now and then, she looked at me too and smiled. Even from across the pool. Like she knew I was looking. Or maybe, she was looking too. Her presence said more than words could. It felt as if peace was flowing through her.

The day flew by in a haze of sun, laziness, and my Spotify playlist blasting through the hotel speakers, courtesy of a kind staff member who just said, "Go on, DJ."

By evening, we were debating dinner plans when Sandra, Shane's aunt, grinned at me and said, "Lukas, go ask that Italian group where is nice local restaurant. You talk to everyone anyway."

She was right, so off I went. The guy didn't speak English, but the girl beside him, the one I'd noticed earlier, leaned in and said, "Two hundred meters along the beach, lovely restaurant, great food."

Back at reception, I asked Eros. He was the receptionist at the hotel if he knew the place and could book us a table for ten. A few minutes later, he looked up from the phone with an apologetic smile. "Kitchen's closed for repairs, but they'll do tapas and drinks. Or..." his grin widened, "we could order pizza to be delivered there." I agreed without hesitation.

Eros was one of those gentle souls that every hotel dreams of having, helpful, smiling, positive and always ready with a solution.

When I arrived at the restaurant to catch the sunset, the place was packed. I came to the bar and asked one of the waitresses if we had a table ready. The waitress asked where the rest of my group was. "On their way... very slowly," I said. I asked her about the pizza. She agreed to the pizza plan but said we'd have to eat it on the beach. That rule lasted about ten minutes before the staff decided we were too entertaining to send away. Ten pizzas, too many cocktails, and a piña colada shortage later, we were well settled in.

At one point, I was chatting with a waitress and mentioned that I was writing a book. She smiled, disappeared for a moment, and returned holding a folded piece of paper.

"We found this letter on a couch today. Is any of you called Thomas?"

I hesitated. "Yes...?" We had Thomas in our group. I called him to come over. The waiter said, "It's from some girl. In English. You're the only ones who speak English here, so... maybe it's for you, maybe it belongs in your book."

I held it for a moment, the paper warm from the waitress's hand, as if it had waited for me. I opened it, didn't know what to expecting.

The paper was folded neatly, the edges soft from being handled. I could tell it had been there for a while, waiting.

I read on, the words simple yet heavy, as if the writer had poured something real into them. She spoke about a night they once shared, how it had stayed in her mind long after. About missing the way he listened to her. About wishing she'd said more, or maybe less.

It wasn't a love letter in the way most people think. There were no grand confessions, no promises. Just truth. Words that felt like they were written for someone who mattered, even if only for a short time.

As I read those words, I couldn't help but feel a quiet wish rise inside me, that maybe, one day, I might meet someone to hear words like these from. Words carrying the kind of feeling that leaves no doubt you've touched someone's heart in a way that stayed.

By the time I finished, I was sitting there in silence, my drink melting beside me. I didn't know Thomas. I didn't know the girl who had written it, yet somehow, holding that letter in my hands, I felt like I'd been trusted with something, as if the universe had passed me a message not entirely meant to miss me.

I realised I was holding more than a stranger's memory. I was holding a mirror.

The words she wrote to him felt so good to read maybe because no one had ever said words like that to me before, and for the first time, I understood how it could feel to read something like this.

Maybe that's why they found me, to show me what it looks like when a heart finally speaks.

Maybe something else wanted to speak to me through this letter.

The man it was meant for would never know how beautifully someone had opened their heart for him. He never received the message, and the girl, perhaps she was too shy to say it aloud. Maybe she missed the moment, and he was gone.

Or maybe she simply didn't want to carry it in her heart anymore, so she wrote it down as if speaking directly into his eyes.

Maybe the letter was a quiet whisper, meant for me, don't change who you are, and when the time is right… don't be afraid.

I looked back at the waitress. She was still smiling, watching for my reaction.

"Strange, isn't it?" she said.

I nodded. "Yes… strange…and maybe a little beautiful."

I folded the paper again and slipped it into my pocket, not because it was meant for me, but because something in it was. Behind me, the sea breathed against the shore, pizza boxes rustled in the breeze, and glasses clinked as laughter rose. For a moment, it felt as if everything had leaned in close, listening too.

The In**V**itation

*I*t was the next morning, just a day before we were meant to leave this beautiful, peaceful place.

As always, after breakfast, I went straight to the pool for some quiet. After a few slow swims up and down, the Italians began to gather.

Then something happened, and I still don't know why it was me. Sara, one of the girls from the group, stopped me and asked, "Would you like to come to our wedding?"

At first, I said yes. Then I asked, "When is the wedding?"

She smiled. "Tomorrow."

I went quiet. Fear whispered all the reasons why I couldn't go. So, I replied, "Sorry, I can't. We're leaving tomorrow."

She asked again, "Would you like to come for lunch at least, tomorrow, with us?"

I asked, "What time?"

She replied, "11 a.m."

I told her I was really sorry, but we were leaving early in the morning, around 9 a.m. I said I'd love to, that I really appreciated the invitation, and that I felt honoured… but unfortunately, I couldn't.

Still, I wanted to do something. So, I went to the bar to buy them at least some prosecco for the celebration, a little gift from me.

On the way to the bar, something inside me whispered... you can't lose if you try.

Even if it makes no sense but if you don't try, the answer will always be no.

A stranger had invited me to a wedding.

I was supposed to work Friday.

I didn't have a hotel.

I didn't have a flight, but I decided to try.

When I brought the prosecco, I turned to Sara with a smile and said, "Look, I'll try. I'll message my boss to see if I can get the day off Friday, check if there's a room available in the hotel, and look for a flight later in the weekend. If I get all three yeses, I'll come."

First, the day off was approved.

Then, against all odds, the receptionist found me a room.

As for the flight? I got one for Sunday.

Three locks.

Three keys.

Two hours later, I came back to the Italian group and said to Sara, with excitement, "Yes, I'm coming!"

They all shouted "Yes!" and handed me a glass of prosecco to toast. My feeling? I don't even know what I felt first in that moment...happiness, excitement, magic...but I know I felt something real. Suddenly, I wasn't just going to a wedding. I was stepping into something else.

Before I left that morning, Sara told me there would be a little gathering, some drinks by the swimming pool later that night, and said that I was welcome to come over if I wanted. I said I would, but we had plans for our last night with my Irish family. We were going out for dinner. She said, "Come after, it's okay."

Later, I shared the news with everyone in our group. Shane started laughing and said, "Lukas, this kind of thing... only happens to you." We laughed, thinking about all my wild stories that somehow always find their way to me.

That evening, when I returned to the hotel, a few guys were already gathered around the groom, drinking. Some people were outside by the swimming pool. The groom saw me and called out my name. We didn't understand each other's language, but we knew how to drink a shot. I bought him and myself a double of whatever he had been drinking, but the other lads laughed and told me I had to drink it straight.

The stress melted off me. It all felt so natural being with them, around them.

I walked down toward the pool and saw Michela, the girl whose insistent energy had caught me earlier, sitting at a table with a few others. I gently approached her and asked if I could sit beside her. Then I asked if it was okay to play a song. She smiled and said, "Of course."

I tried to play something Italian, but of course I didn't know many Italian songs. Then I handed her my phone and asked if she could play some Italian music on Spotify. She didn't just play a song, she sang *L'emozione non ha voce*.

I didn't just hear it. I felt it. Through her voice, the emotion I had been carrying, the one I couldn't find words for, finally spoke. Even if I didn't understand the lyrics, I understood something deeper. It was like her voice was a siren's song, not to lure me, but to awaken something within.

I remember looking at her in that moment. Her eyes, deep brown and warm ... and so was her soul. No walls, only light, honesty. Her beauty wasn't the kind that asked for attention. It felt shaped by goodness, untouched by the bad of the world, and yet seemed unaware of the rare gift she carried.

We played a few more songs, and somewhere between the music and conversation, she said something so random, yet it made me pause. "If you're ever in Naples... call me."

I smiled and replied, "To give you a call, I'll need your number."

She looked at me, calm and soft, and said, "I will give you my number." No pressure. No pretending. Just something true, softly said.

I told her I had once planned to relocate to the Netherlands, but that idea was gone. Still, I had the feeling I needed to leave Ireland, to start fresh somewhere new, though I didn't know the place yet.

Maybe it was a small sign, like a whisper, that Naples was the place I still must see.

When she was leaving back to her room, she looked back at me with a soft smile. "Good night," she said.

"See you tomorrow at the wedding."

Mattia, one of the guys, stayed a little longer with me. We talked about life, exchanged stories, and strangely, it didn't feel like talking to a stranger. There was no small talk, no pretending, just an openness and a flow. Like speaking to someone you've known for many years.

I asked him how he knew the bride and groom. He told me that Sara and Michela were his sisters.

I smiled and said, "Well, I couldn't have talked to better people today. Brother and sister of the bride."

That night in the hotel, her words echoed in my mind. *Come visit Naples.*

Was it just a moment? Was it random? Or was it a sign, a spark of light in the sea to follow, to visit Naples for a reason I didn't yet know?

Maybe some people aren't just passing through. Maybe they arrive like echoes, guiding you toward where you're meant to go, to see, to remember.

Maybe sometimes there are no reasons. You just have to let it flow, to follow and trust without questioning, without knowing why.

Sometimes life shows you the place
long before it shows you the reason.

WhEn Magic invites yoU in

The next morning my best friends left, and I stayed. I cried when I saw them go. We waved not as goodbye, but still… they are like family to me, and this journey will remain unforgettable. I missed their smiles, their voices, their presence beside me. That sense of belonging we created together.

Then, just like that, the day became mine alone.

Standing in front of the hotel, dressed for a wedding I had never expected to attend, I took a deep breath and stepped into the unknown. I was a little nervous, not because of the wedding or the people, but because of the language I didn't know.

Something was arriving softly, patiently, ready for me to live it. Happy tears. Memories of the beautiful people I met, the place that felt like love, the couple who shared that love. It all came together.

It was unplanned. Unexpected. Born from following my voice, not fear. From trusting the signs, not logic. Because I tried and didn't give up, the universe showed me the beauty of surrender.

It began in my room. A cleaner returned my white clothes, freshly washed, the shirt perfectly ironed. While dressing, I showed her two options for my trousers, ankles lifted length or full length. Even without words, we understood each other. She pointed to the lifted length ankles. I put on the shirt and showed her the full outfit.

She smiled.

"Bellissimo."

Three more cleaners came in, and I showed them too. I felt their kindness and warmth, as if I truly belonged there. When I left the room, they all waved the kind of wave that said… don't worry. You've got this.

In the lobby, guests were gathering. I felt a little lost until Clara, Mattia's girlfriend, came over with a smile, spoke to me, brought me to the others I'd met before, and the nervousness melted away. They made me feel like one of them.

I wanted to give the couple a gift, so I asked Eros for an envelope. He couldn't find one, but he made one for me and said, "Lukas, you should write something from your heart." The words came easily, like I'd known them for years.

After one last drink, we boarded the buses. In my minibus there were only three others, but that didn't stop me from playing music from my phone. It wasn't loud, but music always carries its own magic.

Then we arrived at the church.

The air was hot, the kind that clings to your skin. I was grateful for the hand fan I'd brought. The church was breathtaking. Stone walls that had stood for centuries held the cool scent of incense. The light through the high windows was soft and golden, falling across the pews like a blessing.

The bride stepped into the light, dressed in white, her gown flowing softly as she walked toward the man of her life. She was radiant, not just in beauty but in presence. When the groom saw her, you could feel his happiness, not just see it in his smile. It was in the way his whole face lit up, as if nothing else in the world mattered. She walked toward him with the grace of someone moving toward her home, each step a promise, each glance a story only they knew.

It was a beautiful moment, one that seemed to hold the entire church still, as if even time wanted to watch.

After the ceremony, congratulations and a few drinks, we returned to the buses for the next part of the celebration. I pointed to the front seat beside the driver and he nodded. The road ahead wound forty-five minutes into the hills. I leaned toward him and said one word, while pointing to the radio, "Bluetooth?"

He grinned, pointed to the microphone hanging beside me.

"Microfone."

We didn't understand each other's language, but we understood the meanings. In moments, the quiet bus had become a moving disco climbing higher, voices singing along as the road curved between valleys and rising peaks.

It felt like walking into a place from a dream, the kind people talk about, but you never really believe exists. A hidden gem surrounded by mountains.

The air was warm and soft, carrying the light scent of flowers. Paths of smooth marble and stone wound between olive trees and tall palms. Small lights lined the steps, leading up to gardens and fountains. Golden arches stood over walkways, some holding crystal chandeliers that swayed gently in the evening breeze.

In the daylight, it was bright and elegant, at night, it turned into something magical. Palm trees glowed with lights wrapped around their trunks, their reflections shining in the still blue water of the pool. Lanterns flickered along the paths. Strings of tiny bulbs hung above, like a ceiling of stars.

Food and drinks were everywhere, like a celebration that didn't know where to end. Tables overflowed with colours. There were stations for wine, prosecco, cocktails with glasses ready to be picked up and toasted. Everywhere I turned, there was something new to taste, something new to see. It wasn't just a meal. It felt like the place itself was feeding us.

It was peaceful, full of love and the kind of place you don't find often. It didn't just look beautiful, it felt almost unreal, like a scene from a movie, but somehow, it was right there in front of me and as I stood there, taking it all in, I realised this was it. The magic I had felt waiting for me all day had arrived without announcement or force. It was simply here, wrapped in warm air, golden light, and the quiet joy of love.

Then we were called to the main building for dinner. I didn't know where my place was or which table to go to. My name wasn't on the guest list.

Mattia came over to me and said, "You're going to sit with us at our table."

I don't know if I should take it as a coincidence, but the table number was 11.

I was happy to see Michela right beside me. She helped me with all the dinner choices since I had no idea what was on the menu. I couldn't even finish one glass of wine because it was always refilled. It felt like the waitress was hidden somewhere, just waiting for the moment to top it up again.

The guests were a mix of family and friends, each carrying their own kind of joy. Some were elegant in long gowns and dark suits, their laughter soft and warm. Others were lively, glasses always in hand, filling the air with stories and bursts of laughter. There were the quiet ones too, sitting back and watching it all, smiling as if they were guarding the moment. Together, they created a feeling that was more than a celebration, it was a living circle of warmth around Sara and Gaetano, the married couple.

I watched Sara and Gaetano weave through the tables, their smiles as warm as the evening air, stopping to greet each guest as if they'd known them for years. When they reached me, they didn't just ask if everything was okay. They leaned in, listened, their eyes holding mine with the type of kindness that feels rare. It was a small moment, but in a country where I barely spoke the language, it felt like being claimed by family.

I remember their first dance so clearly. It was beautiful. They shone like two souls who had finally found each other, each filling the other's heart. I didn't even know them. I had almost forgotten little moments like that, but they reminded me in the best possible way.

After the first dance, the party began. Everyone was dancing. Some people from a distance, others gathered in the centre around the couple, celebrating with smiles. The night was long, yet it passed so quickly.

At one moment, I walked up to Michela and took her hand to dance. The day of the wedding, she wore a dress that moved with her, not just on her, but part of her. It was strange in the most beautiful way. We danced as if we had been practising together for years. I don't know if the song was long, but the dance with her felt endless. In the quiet space between the music, our eyes met and we smiled. I can't explain it exactly, but it felt like I could feel her, and somehow, she could feel me. The movements were natural, our bodies following the same rhythm, making the same steps, as if we were two dance partners who had been waiting for this moment all along.

As all beautiful moments must pass, this one did too. Only so a better one can come, if you let it. If you let yourself be free, free to choose, free to feel, free to trust. If you believe in yourself and walk into the unknown with a smile, same as I did.

After the celebration, I felt it. The ending was near. Not in a sad way, but in a way that felt complete. As if the book was closing itself, gently, with nothing left to force.

It was unforgettable. The kind of presence that stays in your heart. Not because of how it looked, but because of what it awakened inside. Feelings last far longer than moments ever can.

One day, I hope I'll see the video from that wedding, not only as a memory but as a reminder of how blessed I was to be part of something rare.

I don't know why I was invited, or why they chose me, but they made me feel like part of their family. Maybe I was just lucky and maybe you are too, you just don't see it yet. These are the moments when we question why, when instead we should simply believe. Magic does not choose only a few. It waits for anyone brave enough to see it, and to let it in.

The Night I Belonged

The next day I woke up later than usual. It had been a long night. As always, I went down to the swimming pool. Only a few minutes later, Antonio, one of the guys from the wedding, came over to me.

He asked if I had any plans for the evening, and if I'd like to join him and his family for dinner so I wouldn't be alone. Of course, I had no plans and I happily accepted. He told me we'd meet for dinner at 7 p.m., so it was settled.

Later in the day, more people came over to say goodbye. As I watched each of them leave, I wondered if this was the last time I would see them, or if we would meet again. I hugged everyone, even those I hadn't spoken with much at the wedding. The night had been too short, but I was grateful I could meet such beautiful souls.

When lunchtime came, I had pizza on my mind, nothing else. I asked Eros if he could order one for me. After making a call, he told me I'd have to collect it myself, and it was too far to walk in the heat. I asked if we could call a taxi, but he shook his head. No taxi would come that far from Agrigento just to pick me up for pizza. Then, as always, he had an idea.

He offered me his scooter.

"Have you ever ridden one?" he asked.

"Well," I laughed, "maybe twenty years ago."

We both laughed, but he gave me clear instructions on how to start, showed me where the brakes were, and gave me directions on how to park it safely. When I drove off, I think he was praying for me, because the way I left, I must have looked like a drunk driver. Luckily, once I got onto the road, I found my balance. I wasn't chasing speed, but I could manage.

When I arrived at the restaurant to collect the pizza, I couldn't unclip the helmet. So, I walked in with it still on. The lady inside greeted me with a "Buongiorno" and then asked, "Luca?"

I froze. How could she know my name? Then I realised Eros must have called ahead, worried if I'd even survive the trip.

I asked her for help with the helmet, and though my Italian was broken, she understood me. She laughed and kindly helped me out. On the way back, I felt like a pro, riding the scooter as if I'd been doing it all my life.

Back at the hotel, I thanked Eros for everything, especially for trusting me with his scooter. Somehow, our talk turned deeper, and the words he spoke are ones I'll never forget, he said, "I've been doing this job for ten years. I've met thousands and thousands of clients in my life. I don't think I've ever met such an extraordinary person as you. I don't think I ever will."

I tried to hold back my tears. To hear such words from a stranger felt like a gift. Words are powerful. They can break you sometimes, but they can also lift you up, make you believe in yourself in a way you know deep down but never say out loud.

The rest of the afternoon, I relaxed in my room.

At 7 p.m. I met Antonio, but he told me the plans had changed slightly. If I didn't mind. At 9 p.m. we would first watch a video the couple's friends had prepared for them, together with family and close friends, and then go for dinner. I was honoured.

We gathered in the hotel's main hall. The video played with captured memories of the bride and groom since their childhood. People laughed, people cried. Messages rolled in from friends and family. I didn't even understand Italian, but somehow, I felt the words.

When the video finished, we walked together to dinner, to the same restaurant where I'd had pizza earlier. The lady who had helped me with the helmet was still there. The moment she saw me, we both started laughing. Only the two of us knew why.

A long table was set up for us, around twenty people. I was seated beside Michela. Somehow ever since that first day, I always seemed to end up by her side. Once we all got our food and everyone began to eat, I looked around. It was like a scene from a movie… people talking, smiling, passing the wine, sharing food, telling their stories, and me? I can't explain it, but I felt like I was a part of it. It felt like these weren't strangers I had just met, but as if I had known them all my life.

After dinner, a plan I hadn't known about became apparent. Michela asked if I wanted to join them at a party or go back with the "older ones." Of course, I said yes to the party.

We piled into three cars. The married couple couldn't join us, as they were leaving early the next morning for their honeymoon. On the road, it felt like a concert. Michela and two others sang loudly all the way to the party.

At the entrance, I was told not to speak. "Tonight, your name is Gaetano," they joked. I guessed the party was only for people on the list. Somehow, we all got in.

We danced all night, the last to leave. On the way back, the car was still a nightclub, Michela and the others performing their "afterparty concert" without pause.

When we arrived at the hotel, the couple were just leaving for their honeymoon. We gave them warm hugs and in that time, I realised

I might not see these people again, the ones I celebrated a wedding with, shared a family dinner with, and danced alongside all night. I wasn't sad, I knew these memories would stay with me forever. Sometimes the most beautiful part of life is not knowing if you'll meet again but knowing you were lucky enough to meet at all.

I left with something I can never lose… a reminder that home is not always a place, but the moments when you feel accepted as you are.

The Last Day in Sicily

The next morning, I woke up early, knowing it was my last day in a place that had given me so much. I looked around the room and slowly started packing my things. Leaving, but not really ready to leave. The memories surrounded me like a soft kind of magic, the kind your heart doesn't want to walk away from.

I felt something I couldn't quite name. A little sadness, a little gratitude, and a quiet ache for everything I had to leave behind, but also for everything I now carried within me.

I went for breakfast, then walked down to the swimming pool. That's where Michela and I had agreed to meet. She was staying longer but offered to leave with me by bus. We had agreed to meet around 11 a.m., as it was late when we went to sleep the night before.

Antonio, the man from the wedding with the big heart, arrived first. We spoke using Google Translate, smiling as he told me what time he'd bring us to the bus station.

Then Michela arrived.

We sat by the pool and spoke about life, travel, dreams.

I asked her softly, "What's your biggest dream?"

Her answer didn't shock me. It made me pause.

Not because of the words, but because of how she said them, with a kind of truth that doesn't hide.

She said, "To have a happy family."

In that moment, I felt it. The same dream I've always carried, wanting to live it fully with love at the centre.

Time passed quickly. We spoke a lot, but nothing ever felt rushed. It was like getting to know each other quietly, without needing to perform, just being present and honest no matter the topic.

3 p.m. came. Time to leave the hotel.

She was headed to Catania. I was supposed to go to Palermo.

Then, last minute, I asked, "What would you think if I came with you to Catania Airport? I still have time… my flight's not until Sunday."

She smiled right away. "Yes, of course."

Just like that, a new path opened.

Once Antonio brought us to the bus station, Michela and I had a quick snack before the bus, a two-and-a-half-hour journey ahead.

At the shop, on the way out, Michela asked (thank God she did) which bus stop was for Catania.

We almost missed it. The bus didn't stop where we expected, and we ran the whole way.

When we reached Catania, her flight was delayed an hour.

I asked if she wanted to eat something before take-off.

We went to McDonald's.

She took a call, so I quietly asked what she wanted. Just my luck, she picked exactly what I was going to order.

Not wanting to look like a copycat, I changed the sauce.

Of course, I picked the spicy one, the only thing I can't eat.

It sat there untouched, like a small red flag waving at me while she laughed. I laughed too. The sauce stayed behind, feeling left out.

One of the conversations I remember most came out of nowhere.

It was deeper, about love and belief, like the universe wanted to ask me itself, to see if I still hadn't given up.

She asked me something no one ever had, "Do you really believe in that kind of love?"

The kind that never fades. The kind that burns on the last day just as brightly as on the first.

I looked into her eyes and saw it not just belief, but a quiet hope.

Like she wanted to believe but wasn't sure if it truly existed.

She reminded me of myself when I was her age, twenty years ago.

I told her, "Yes. I believe in that kind of love, a flame that stays lit from the moment you meet until the day you leave this world. Something real. Not regular."

She said, "But I've never heard of anyone who has that."

I answered, "You're right. Because for that kind of love to exist, you need two people who believe in the same magic and so far, I haven't met anyone who believes like I do, yet I know it's out there."

In that moment, a quiet thought rose in my mind not for her ears, only for me.

Like the little boy inside was reminding me...

What if love isn't just emotion? Maybe it's not something we fall into, but something we awaken to.
A whisper from the stars reminding us of a promise made before time had a name.
A thread that weaves through space, through lifetimes, through souls and somehow, you meet each other again.

She also asked something else, soft, out of nowhere, "Do you regret anything from college, from your past mistakes?"

In that quiet moment, I paused.

She reflects on life in a way most people don't dare to slow down for.

Maybe that's why we connected, not just in words, but in essence.

Maybe that moment wasn't about agreement, advice, or even shared experience, but about the fact that we both carry questions. She asked me questions I hadn't dared to ask myself and somehow, we gave each other the space to speak them.

In a world full of people pretending to know what they're doing, maybe the real ones are the ones still quietly wondering. Still pausing. Still listening.

We spent two hours at the airport, and when her boarding time came, I gave her something.

A bracelet I had rebuilt and carried since.

I hadn't planned to give it away, but in that moment, it just felt right.

"I want you to have this," I said. "It will protect your dream. Help it come true."

At first, she didn't want to take it. She knew it meant a lot to me.

I told her I had another to carry.

She smiled and accepted.

Even if we never saw each other again, her dream felt worth protecting, the same dream I've always carried.

It was time to say goodbye.

We stood for a second longer than needed.

Not speaking.

Just letting the moment settle.

After a strong, warm hug, I turned toward the stairs. She began walking toward her gate.

Halfway there, as if pulled by the same thought, we both stopped and looked back.

Our eyes met. No smile, no words. Just that kind of thankful silence that speaks,

like a guide whispering, *don't stop being you. You're going to be exactly where you're meant to be when the time is right.*

Not every story needs a future. Some remind us of what we almost lost.

I no longer live in the illusions of what could be.

I live in the quiet truth of where I stand.

Still, I carry hope not as a fantasy, but as a soft flame.

When something touches me deeply, it stays. Not to hold me back, only to remind me that something real once passed through my life.

She reminded me of something quieter, a warmth that doesn't need to burn to be felt.

A smile that brings peace. A thoughtful answer to a simple question.

For a little while, she reminded me that what I'm looking for is still possible.

Even if it's not now but I know it's out there, waiting for me.

I do not chase. I do not force.

The echo was enough to remind me that I'm not the only one who can feel deeply.

That I can hope, that life always brings what is meant for me, when my heart is ready and when the time is right.

Maybe she was the final touch before I meet someone who looks at the world with the same eyes, someone who understands it fully.

Her presence reminded me of who I have always been, and that in the past someone had tried to take that away from me.

What comes next? I'm not trying to figure that out.

I don't need answers or control over my future anymore. Only to listen to the signs and let my little flame guide me toward the one who's out there, waiting for me.

EPilogue

*A*n Open Heart Survives Everything
Now, as I stand at the edge of this story, I don't feel the need to chase the ending.

Maybe the ending isn't a door closing. Maybe it's the moment you stop running and start seeing what's already here. How easy it is to live too far ahead and forget what's right in front of you.

I am proud of the person who began this journey. Lost sometimes. Broken sometimes, but never giving up, even when everything else fell apart. Without that person, I would not be here now.

I could have closed my heart after everything, but I didn't. I kept it open, even when it hurt. I walked through darkness without losing my light. I believed when it would have been easier not to. I carried hope when the world told me to let it go.

If tears fall while you read these words, let them fall. They are not tears of pain, but of gratitude. Gratitude for the courage it took to keep going, for the faith that carried you here, for the love that never left you.

You made it, and you did it with an open heart. And an open heart survives everything.

From all the stories in my life, this path revealed something else. Something beautiful I had never seen before. Even through the hard things, my heart has grown strong enough to love. I have learned that anger is not the enemy but a defence, and before I turn it outward, I must first learn to understand it.

I forgive the past, not for others but for myself. So, I can smile… and, with a smile, happiness always rises. I could carry anger toward people for what happened, but the truth is it would hurt only one person most, the one I should love instead. Myself.

Not everything makes sense, and not everything needs control. Sometimes you just need to believe that one day you will be exactly where you are meant to be. I have asked many times why it happened to me, but I have learned it is not always about answers. Sometimes it is about acceptance. About letting go.

It was never only about what happened. It was about what remained. The light. The belief. The voice inside that whispers, keep going.

Maybe all the love, all the distance, all the connections across places were the universe teaching me something. Preparing me for the moment when I would finally be ready. Ready for the one I was meant to be with.

Sometimes magic leads us to the most unexpected place. To meet the person we were never expecting, yet somehow always meant to find because patience has its own time, and dreams should never be abandoned.

Because in our dreams, everything remains possible…
and everything that remains possible is already alive in us.

Thank You

To my Mama and my sister for your endless love and belief.
To my friends who became family, for every word of support, laughter, and patience along the way.

To **Joanne**, my proofreader, for treating every page with such care and for helping me keep the voice of my heart intact.

To **Dasha** for guiding the marketing strategy with passion and heart and for capturing the soul of the book through her creative vision and social media work.

To **Itta**, helping me build the website the home where *Something Else* can be found.

Most of all, to you, the reader. Thank you for opening these pages and walking with me through them. You made it here, and that means something.

About the Author

Lukas Simko was born in Slovakia and moved to Ireland while he was still discovering who he was. Since then, life has taken him on unexpected paths across countries, through love and heartbreak, moments of luck, loss, and experiences so unlikely that people often told him, *"You should write a book."*

He is not a polished writer by trade. He studied IT, worked his way through different jobs, and stumbled more times than he can count but writing became his way of telling the truth, not just the facts of what happened but how it felt inside. The doubts, the signs, the laughter, the silence and the moments that cracked him open and showed him something more.

*Life isn't about perfection,
but about loving what's inside you, perfectly imperfect.*

www.ingramcontent.com/pod-product-compliance
Lightning Source LLC
Chambersburg PA
CBHW060454080526
44584CB00015B/1431